BEYOND UPANISHAD

VOLUME 1

Dr Dipak pramanik

Table of Contents

Page No

REVIVAL OF VEDAS AND UPANISHADS THROUGH DIAMOND OR JIBANKRISHNA

"Access to the Vedas is the greatest privilege this century may claim over all previous centuries" – Dr.J.Robert Oppenheimer

Jibankrishna once said, "What has happened here? What is Veda, and what is that Lost Purusha (mentioned in Vedas) – those were lost. Today that has been revived and shown to us. But even Vedas could not clarify the phenomenon of the 'Lost Purusha' clearly, though Upanishads to some extent clarified it. What is the real phenomenon, nobody could say? Even this phenomenon happened long, long years before Vedas. They have only been mentioned on the basis of Sruti (Memorizing the hymns through generations after generations). They could not say that this is the story of human beings. Now this mystery has been exposed to us today.

Listen, after millions of years this Purusha revives."

A FEW WORDS ABOUT WRITING MY BOOK 'UPANISHAD REVIVED'

It was early morning on April 16, 2008, Wednesday.

I had a strange dream: I was seeing an unknown open area which seemed to be of a very far past scene. I was roaming here and there. In one place of a field, I noticed that a group of people sitting on the ground in a circle was chanting some hymns. It was a little bit dark due to the evening time. They were not clearly visible. Sometimes the sound 'Hing' was heard in between the chanting. The sound and the languages were quite unnatural and unusual though it was very melodious. Suddenly a voice was heard near me, 'They are chanting the Vedic hymns.' I realized that another man was with me though I couldn't recognize his presence for so long. Then the dream was off, though the chanting was echoing in my ear throughout the day.

In the evening a quote from Swami Vivekananda flashed in my mind. He said, 'The actual meaning and lyrics of the Vedic hymns are lost. They are not uttered properly. These hymns were properly used to be uttered by the Vedic Rishis and for that reason would manifest in their bodies. But that is a lost chapter now.'

I realized that I heard the accurate musical noting of the Vedic hymns in my dream.

After this dream, it flashed in my mind one day, how will it be if a book on Jibankrishna's spiritual realizations based on Upanishads is written?

This was established in a strange manner after a few months.

On August 28, 2008, when I started writing the book on Jibankrishna with reference to Upanishad, I had to consult Chandogya Upanishad for reference. There is one chapter I read about an incident that perplexed me to a great extent.

In the twelfth chapter of the first volume of Chandogya Upanishad, it is written like this :

Once the son of Dalvya Rishi and the son Bak or Glub of Mitra Rishi went out of their village for studying Vedas.

Then some Rishis in the disguise of white dogs appeared before them and asked them to enchant hymns and to come in the next morning to the same place. So they waited there till the next morning. The Rishis in the disguise of white dogs chanted the Vedic hymns with the utterance of a sound 'Hing' in between the hymns (In the Vedic era during hymns one of the Rishis used to utter this word

'Hing'. This hymn belongs to the seventh Sukta of the ninth Mondal of Rigveda.

The whole dream thus became clear to me and I understood that I saw the same incident described in Chandogya Upanishad though it happened some thousands of years before Upanishads were written. The Upanishads were written some three to four thousand years ago on the basis of memories from generation after generation, while RicVeda was the oldest. But the incidents happened much prior to that.

The effect of the dream was as such. I felt no trouble in searching the references out of 13 Upanishads for my book though this was the first time I read Upanishads translated into English and Bengali from the Sanskrit language.

Whenever I wanted any reference, it took seconds to find the same. This was really astonishing and amazing.

Jibankrishna used to discuss his lifelong divine realizations with innumerable listeners coming to his residence every day. The discussions were mainly based on the metaphors of Sri Ramkrishna as described in the Gospel of Sri Ramkrishna and it used to continue from noontime to night. These discussions and daily experiences were recorded by some listeners in their diaries and later on have been published in a Bengali magazine since 1968. These are compiled in my Bengali book 'Upanishader pare' (beyond Upanishad) and later on, are translated into English.

Lastly, it is noteworthy to mention the nomenclature of this book as 'Jibankrishna Upanishad personified' and 'Beyond Upanishad'. Initially, I had a confusion about keeping this nomenclature. But a dream of Sambhunath Sinha who was a Jibankrishna's companion eliminated my confusion. The dream was thus:

Brother Sambhu was seeing in his dream that his father coming to him was saying, "I was present alone in the primordial age. At that time Vedas and Upanishads were not created and there were no Rishis (Sages). Later on, they had worshiped me."

[Jibankrishna used to mention that during the era of Vedic Rishis they mentioned Almighty God as Father because they used to see God in the form of their father].

His father then said, "Why are you bothering about the nomenclature of the book? The matter is the primary thing and let the same name be kept." Then his dream was off.

Actually brother Sambhu came to know from me about the name of my book and after hearing his dream I was surprised and decided to keep the same name.

ABOUT JIBANKRISHNA OR DIAMOND

I am going to narrate a very strange phenomenon happening since the early part of the 20th century encircling a person named Jibankrishna or Diamond who was born in 1893 at Howrah town adjacent to Kolkata, India.

A boy of 12 years 4 months old, he had no idea about religion. One night Thakur Sri Ramkrishna appeared in his dream. He was lying on his bed. Just as in reality Thakur Sri Ramkrishna standing on his feet began to talk with him. But whom he saw in the dream was completely unknown to him. At 13 years 8 months age he saw Swami Vivekananda, though he was also an unknown person to him. Sitting for the whole night near his head he taught him. At dawn, that form disappeared and a sound flashed within his brain – 'Rajyoga'! This was also the first time that he became acquainted with the word 'Rajyoga'.

At the age of 15 years, he first saw the picture of Thakur Sri Ramkrishna. With great astonishment, he looked at the picture and thought – "Oh, he is Lord Sri Ramkrishna who appears in my dream from time to time"!

Thereafter a chapter of divine realizations and dreams opened in his eyes. It started at the age of 12 years 4 months and continued throughout his life with newer realizations. How many original realizations he had cannot be counted, and no such realizations are found in any religious scriptures. Yet he had no self-exertions, all happened spontaneously. Atman or Self was manifested within him spontaneously. No such thoughts of austerity ever appeared in his mind. Whether God can be visualized or whether it is necessary to cry for visualizing was unknown to him. Never in his life, he worshipped any god or goddess; he knew no hymns; he never offered any flower to the legs of Sri Ramkrishna without whom he knew no other gods or goddesses, what about any ritualistic performances. He used to live the life of an ordinary man and witnessed all these realizations were happening in his life.

Any sensible person can understand what deep revelations occurred within him, how many mysteries of the spiritual world were exposed in his life. Every page of his book is enlightened with his revelations. But still, he never accepted his individualistic austerities. He never paused anywhere by accepting the individualistic austerity as the final Truth of mankind.

Now, he never knew that God can be visualized. Then how did he visualize God? He used to say that a human being is born with innumerable prejudices – these are his or her family prejudice, clan prejudice, country's prejudice, etc. Not only so. Whatever has happened so far on earth all those prejudices are hidden within the brain. Those prejudices are manifested as and when necessary during individualistic austerity. So, who even knows nothing about visualizing God, sees God within. The old prejudice of visualizing God manifests unknowingly within the seer. And so, whatever is true for the seer, if it is not universal and proof cannot be cited, he is not prepared to accept.

Thus with such negation Diamond lived his life. But where he had to stop, it was such that a new chapter opened and that was a universal austerity encircling him. His form began to appear among myriads of people. Innumerable people began to see him in dreams, trance, meditation, and even in a waking state. Hindus see him, Muslims see him,

Jews see him, Christians see him, Parsees see him, Indians as well as foreigners, see him in all the stages of life. Among them some are rich, some are illiterate. After coming to him some people began to see him within them, again some without coming to him, without hearing his name, saw him not only in dreams but also in waking state, and they were innumerable in number. Later on, when they came to him through their companions or for some reason they narrated their visions. Women were not allowed to come to him, yet by sitting in their houses they used to see him in dreams or waking state. A man started coming to him, then gradually his wife, sons, and daughter, even maids started seeing Diamond in dreams. Sometimes any man came to him, but before he saw Diamond in a dream, his wife or mother or any other member of his family started seeing him in dreams or waking state. There is no barrier, no boundary. The only requirement to see him was only the human body.

Those who saw him had so many differences in ages, education, wealth, and realizations. Yet within these diversities, there was unity and the yogic form of that oneness or unity was his form.

Here the individualistic consciousness was transformed into Universal Consciousness. By eliminating individualism he was transformed into Universalism among humanity. Where ever congenial ground was found his form was manifested within a human body whatever religion, gender, or age were there.

"I am one and all" – this has become realistic now. He is one and many. This phenomenon was mentioned in Maitri Upanishad thus:

"When a seer sees the Brilliant,
Maker, Lord, Person the Brahma-source;
Then, being a knower, shaking off good and evil,
He reduces everything to unity in the Supreme Imperishable'. [6.18]

In the material world, he was different but in the spiritual world he was one – "Sa Ekah". Being appeared within a human body he has given the right to everybody to say, "I am that Brahma" (Aham Brahmasmi).

Socrates said, "Absolut Equality and Abstract Equality"; Swami Vivekananda said, "One and Oneness". Whatever picture about the long waited Oneness they have drawn, we are witnessing its initiation in our daily lives.

The prayer of the old Vedic sages uttered thousands and thousands of years ago is now echoed within myriads of people who are seeing this person within their bodies. No doubt we are blessed and fortunate. Where in India it was said by Sankhya Philosophy that the existence of God is proof-less, in the same country the opposite words are now uttered by us that there is proof that God exists. And that God is a living human being. A man is transformed into God and it is proved by the human race.

Svetasvatara Upanishad has mentioned about such Cosmic Person thus:

"Higher than the senses are the objects of sense,
Higher than the objects of senses is the mind;
And higher than the mind is the intellect.
Higher than the intellect is the Great Self (Atman).
Higher than the Great is the Unmanifest (avyakta),
Higher than the Unmanifest is the Person.
Higher than the Person there is nothing at all.
That is the goal. That is the highest course". [3.10-11]

PART 1 – JIBANKRISHNA OR DIAMOND THE PERSONIFIED UPANISHAD

This Purusha (Person) is mentioned in the Upanishad. He is universal, omnipresent in all beings, and eternal. Such a person cannot be defined judicially. Upanishad is the only authentic source of Brahma. All the information about Brahma is found in Upanishads. So, this Person is termed as personified Upanishad. Brihad Aranyaka Upanishad has mentioned such a person like this:

Brahma – The Cosmic Person with the physical body

In Brihad Aranyaka Upanishad a progressive attempt was made to conceive of Brahma. It was admitted that Brahma was to be found not only in the not-Self but also in the Self; that it was not only the essence of Cosmical phenomena but also of the organic and mental functions of the human person.

This probably was an outgrowth of the macrocosmic conception of an enormous human person. [2.1]

REVIVAL OF UPANISHAD AFTER THOUSANDS OF YEARS IN JIBANKRISHNA'S ERA

On 21.6.1962 Jibankrishna said,"Rig Veda says. 'He who dwells in a man and he who dwells in the sun are one and the same. This might be experienced some thousands of years ago. So they could say like this. Does it mean that thousands and thousands of years rolled by and none during this period had this experience? And these experiences are being achieved by so many people after such a long time and why did this happen to me? Who am I? I am the most ordinary man like you. I have understood that my brain power is increased

VEDIC RISHIS COULD NOT MENTION THE REALIZATIONS OF FIVE SHEATHS OR SEVEN PLANES WHICH WERE MANIFESTED IN JIBANKRISHNA

On 15.10.1960 Jibankrishna discussed:

It is unfathomable how many infinite attributes and power a human body bears. See, this austerity of the five sheaths have been manifested within my body step by step, Vedas have mentioned only about five sheaths or seven steps but they couldn't say about the realizations of every sheath or plane. Why? Because their bodies did not permit.

This visualization of Atma or Self– I had it within this body: The universe within Atma, the universe becomes seed that occurred within this body. The seed becomes a dream; Then the dream vanishes --all these happened in my body. Then seeing my form within your body – so long I have been hearing from your mouth. Now for several months, I have started seeing you within me. How many more attributes this human body bears cannot be conceived. Now one question you can raise – whether those attributes belong to this physical body or the divine consciousness of this body? But listen, you cannot discard this physical body, because without this physical body the consciousness cannot exist and be seen. So it won't do that you will consider only consciousness. The carnal, pulp, seed, everything should be considered. Now my body is a human body. When you see my form, do you see my consciousness? My whole body is divine consciousness and that one you see within you. But is it the end? No there are more. Even if you judge it for unlimited years, you cannot fathom it. There is another explanation – Each and every human being has got his own attributes, but all are merging into one attribute – He is one – 'Sah Ekah' (Veda). So there is no end to it.

[Chhandogya Upanishad (8.12.3) says:

"And thus this blessed one rising upward from within the physical sheath is transformed into the Supreme light and he by appearing in his very identical living form as a man-made of God's light within the bodies of numberless people evinces his attainment of the Supreme light."

Jibankrishna explained on the basis of his revelation:

The form appearing within myriads of people is called Atma, Abhayam and Brahma. This is the eternal truth....

Rising upward from within the physical sheath of the blessed one or Samprasada."

To rise upward and to get oneself transformed into the Supreme light means to pass through five sheaths or Koshas and seven planes.

Five Koshas:-

1) Annamaya Kosha is the gross physical body.

2) Pranamaya Kosha is the sheath where the vital force accumulates and is seen.

3) Monomaya Kosha is at the heart.

4) Vijnamaya Kosha starts from the throat and comprises the seventh plane where God is shown by the man who comes down from the Brahmapura.

5) Anandamaya Kosha is the sheath where the Samprasada changes into bliss alone. Furthermore, there are seven planes in the five Koshas.

They are:-

1) Annamaya Kosha has got no plane.

2) Pranamaya Kosha has got three planes.

They are:-

a) Organ of generation;

b) Organ of evacuation;

c) The navel (abdominal region)

Experience-- Bluish gurgling water with moonbeams dancing therein is seen in the right of the abdomen. The human body is the earth element and water is another element that has separated from it.

3) Heart is the fourth plane called Monomaya Kosha and here the light is seen.

Experience-- Radiant light or fire is seen.

Fire-- another element. In the Vedic term, the whole course of manifestation and transformation is called Agni-Vidya.

4) Vijnanamaya Kosha has got three planes- fifth, sixth, and seventh.

Experience of the fifth plane-

a) Ardhanariswara-- half man and half woman.

b) The sky is seen. The sky is seen within the same as the sky is seen on the outside.

Experience of the sixth plane-

a) Two circles (of light) come out. One from each eye settles to become one in the middle of the eyebrows, which is the Jnananetra or the eye of knowledge.

b) The mysterious Maya in the form of an exquisitely beautiful woman of a light blue complexion and dressed in pansy blue dancing in a slow rhythmical measure, with the tip of the thumb resting in the middle of the eyebrow and eyes looking down, her person exuding heavenly bliss all around.

c) Radiance of a rising sun behind a thin silken curtain. So we find one sun in the sky outside and another sun in the cerebrum inside. The Universe and the human body both tally here.

Experience of the seventh plane is God as shown by God-the-Preceptor who descends in human form from Brahmapura (that is the cerebrum). At this stage special knowledge dawns on the seer- he comes to know that he is God. Here we find that the seer becomes identical with God and the Universe.]

VEDIC RISHIS DID NOT DESCRIBE THE VISUALIZATION OF GOD WHEREAS IN JIBANKRISHNA IT HAPPENED STEP BY STEP

On 23.4.1961 Jibankrishna said,

"See, Rishis said, 'you visualize Self or Atman.' But he did not say, 'Visualize God.' What is the cause? Can you say what is God? Why they did not utter about God? Soul or Atman is emanated from this body. This Life Power of the human body is concentrated in the cerebrum and seen – that is God. See, I had all these experiences very elaborately and then what you are doing? You have carried that proof to me. I have said nothing. On the contrary, you are saying what is God. However, why Rishis have not uttered anything about God? As they had no experience on the austerity of Soul. So how could they say about God?

Jibankrishna vividly described the steps for visualizing God or Atman or Great Soul in his book 'Religion and Realization' as such:

The process of transformations of the five sheaths from one into another takes place. From the human body, the life-power separates, comes up, accumulates, and transforms into a mental plane with pure faculty of seeing God's light in him as well as in the outer world. This transformation goes on till it turns into Bliss. It is an emanation and the manifestation of God with attributes in the body.

There are seven planes which are the seats of these five sheaths and each plane has got its separate manifestation and realization of God in the body. It cannot be seen by vivisection. It can be visualized in 'Bhagavati Tanu' (causal body), the human form which grows within the body, and it is made of God's light. Pranamaya Kosha (Sheath) has got three planes – (a) organ of generation; (b) organ of evacuation; (c) At the naval. In the case of Pranamaya Kosha Sri Ramkrishna says, 'When water oozes out from the 'Alek lata', an invisible creeper, and gets into the abdomen, then a tree grows'. He said in such a manner that nobody understands. Can you say why he has not mentioned the planes and what does he mean by the tree?

What I have written about this meaning is such – 'God without any form (Nirguna Brahma – the Absolute) lying in and through the body, has entwined it like an invisible creeper. He, out of sheer mercy, releases Himself from the body and percolates in the right side of the abdomen. It is seen. It looks like light bluish gargling water mingled with peaceful sparkling moonbeams. And I saw it within my body.

Then comes Manomaya Kosha (Sheath comprising of the fourth plane – the heart.

About the experience on this plane, Sri Ramkrishna said that goddess Kali showed him that every article, including the door, door-steps, ceilings, etc had been saturated with God's light. But why did no other people see it? There were about a hundred maids in the temple and the villagers also used to come to the temple, but none saw it. Were all of them blind?

On a higher sphere we shall get its real meaning – Through my own consciousness, I shall see the world in divine consciousness. I have written my experience thus: This is the first plane where God's light is manifested and seen. On whatever side you may turn your eyes, you will find God's light pervading everything coming within you ken. For instance, you turn your eyes and gaze at the branch of a tree and your eyes will meet the light like molten silver or mercury pervading the branch. Then comes Vijnanamaya Kosha (Sheath comprising the fifth plane, the sixth plane, and a portion of the seventh plane).

In Vijnanamaya Kosha springs up the consciousness of the Real self and it is revealed – 'Who I am'!' God releases Himself from the body and undergoing several kinds of transformations, ultimately takes the form of Atma (soul). The seer having all these sportive forms of God in his own body becomes conscious that he is not the body, but he is Atma.

The fifth plane has its seat in the throat. What I have mentioned about its manifestation and realization within me?

The seer will see himself that his body is transformed into half-woman and half-man. The lower portion is a woman and the upper portion is a man. The condition lasts for two to three minutes. It happens in broad daylight and the seer sees it. This realization makes the seer conscious that Atma (soul) is neither a woman nor a man.

This is the first condition when animal passion (lust) commences evaporating from the body. God is in the body. He releases Himself from the body, assumes the form of half-woman and half-man, and makes you see this with eyes wide open in broad daylight.

The location of the sixth plane is in the middle of the two eyebrows on the forehead.

What I have recorded about my experiences? From the eyes come out two small circles, half-inch in diameter, and having the surface covered with God's light, they rise upwards to the eyebrows and stop there. They unite, become one, and vanish. In no time a single circle appears in their place, Now, the circle in it bears the insignia of knowledge – such as a small Buddha in meditation, and the image of Buddha indicates the realization to come in the seventh plane. This circle is called the Jnana Netra, third eye, or Eye of Knowledge.

At the gate to the entrance of the seventh plane, Sahashrara, the living form of an exquisitely beautiful young lady is seen. She is the image of the mysterious Maya.

Maya is the goddess who keeps a man in separation from God.

It is broad daylight. The seer is lying flat on his bed with eyes wide open. He sees the lady. Her complexion is light blue, but shining just like a bluish pansy. Her apparel is of the color of the sky. At the end of her nose on one side, there is a small gem fixed. Her gaze is bent and fixed on the ground. The thumb of the right hand is placed in the middle of her eyebrows. She is dancing. The dance is of very slow motion but charmingly rhythmical. She seems to be made of joy and bliss. This joy and bliss come down from her body and flood the earth. Her bent and fixed gaze reveal that she is the keeper of the mystery of this human life, the world of God. All kinds of realizations on the way to seeing and becoming god are but vivisection of this Maya. The Supreme knowledge of Brahmajnan lies in solving the mystery of 'Life and Death'.

The next realization is in the seventh plane but it has been mentioned grossly. My experience was beyond this plane and I have recorded it thirteen years back – A hanging silken curtain was seen and beyond it, the Aurora with a rising sun.

Next comes the visualization of God. This is seen in the seventh plane.

The life-power of the Blessed one (Samprasad) reaches the seventh plane. Here God is seen. It is called the 'Triputy' or the threefold. This is the very Trinity of Christianity. This Triputy three-fold stage in the cerebrum or the seventh plane has got three different phases; they are –

1) Jnana the knowledge, that is the Personified giver of the knowledge. He is nobody else but the very person who came down from the 'Brahmapura'or the cerebrum or if for the first time he appears now, then he is an unknown one. But the second one is very defective as this experience is very weak and it is reckoned and accepted in the Vedas.

2) Jneya – the object to be known; this object is nothing else but God Himself.

3) Jnata – the knower.

A limitless ocean of light, very pleasing one, very soothing one, as if an ocean of charm. Over this ocean or one side stands the Person who came down from the Brahmapura (cerebrum). He takes up his right hand, stretches the forefinger, points to a thumb-like appearance but is marked and encircled by a very delicate line of bluish light over the ocean of the light, and speaks, 'This is God! This is seeing of the God!'

Within the thumb-like appearance, the knower and the object to be known are both combined. The knower sees everything and hears everything from within the thumb-like appearance. Now the Person of the Brahmapura (cerebrum) melts in it.

Then the consciousness of the Blessed one comes back and each and every iota of the scene and occurrence is remembered; and up to the date, it is vividly evergreen in His memory.

No more it is confined to the Blessed individual (Samprasada), but furthermore, the Blessed one has become transformed into the Supreme one. His stage is the sixth plane, i.e., the causal body or the Vijnanamaya Kosha in each and every member of the human race. The Vedic lore runs thus 'Swena Rupena Avinispadyate' and again in the Brahmasutra, 'Sampadyah Abirvabha'. The translation comes to this – the proof of the attainment of this Brahmahood will be corroborated by the appearance in the very form made of the light of God of the attainer in the innumerable people. Chandyogya Upanishad points out that not even twenty thousand hold Him but He is boundless and limitless. The attainer of the Brahmahood will be seen by numberless people within their own bodies. The attainer himself will also see almost all within himself, whosoever will come in contact with him. The attainer of the Brahmahood clarifies and bears proof of the aphorism – 'One is All and All is One.' The translation of the Vedic stanza is this – 'Thousands will see him within themselves and He shall see thousands within Him. This is the peculiar characteristic of the Parama Brahma (Supreme Being) and nothing else.'

This is the most mysterious feature of the miracle as it is nothing but the most insurmountable miracle for one Man to be seen by myriads of men as long as he lives.

Every human being has got an innate Brahmahood within him. Sometimes this Brahmahood unfolds itself bears its proof 'you have become universal'. And the Truth is a perennial one, as spoken in the Vedas.

Taittiriya Upanishad has mentioned about such a person going through the realizations of five sheaths as such:

"He performed austerity. Having performed austerity, he understood that Brahma to bliss. For truly, indeed, beings here are born from bliss, when born they live by bliss, on deceasing they enter into bliss". [3.6]

Regarding visualizing half woman and half man in the fifth plane by Diamond and the realization that Soul or Atma is neither woman nor man. Svetasvetara Upanishad has mentioned reincarnating individual soul like this:

"Not female, nor yet male is it; Nor yet is this neuter, whatever body he takes to himself, with that he becomes connected". [5.10]

The effect of visualizing Atma or the Soul is described by Brihad Aranyaka Upanishad as such:

"He who has found and has awakened to the soul (self)
The world is his; indeed, he is the world itself." [4.4.13]

JIBANKRISHNA'S REALIZATIONS ARE BEYOND THE FIVE SHEATHS MENTIONED IN UPANISHADS

On 21.3.1960 Jibankrishna discussed:

For a few days, some bubbles of thoughts are appearing in my brain. Why Vedas have mentioned the five sheaths or seven planes? But I saw that there were many more sheaths and the realizations of those sheaths were manifested in me. But as they have mentioned only those sheaths, so I have mentioned to you about those sheaths. Though they have only mentioned the sheaths, they have not mentioned the realizations. And I have mentioned my realizations so vividly and clearly so many times. But do you know what has happened? I have such realizations which do not come under any of those heaths. For example, the mysterious 'Maya Murti' (dancing lady)! What is the sheath of that realization? Thus I have so many realizations which do not come under any of those sheaths

THE VEDIC TRUTH MANIFESTED IN JIBANKRISHNA

Jibankrishna stated as such:

The very Vedic Truth as experienced in one's life is going to be related to its full-fledged form; how it works in a man and what experiences are made when the goal is attained. It is personal experiences narrated. And thus, it is Truth. And the veracity of this personal Truth will be corroborated when it becomes universal as spoken in the Vedas. By the form of the experienced man, it proves its own Truth and this form will appear within the body of innumerable men, women, and children. It is meant for each and every man, boy, and old alike. It is en-masse, as the attainer of the Supreme Light in the cerebrum is the Universalle-La-Homme. It is this 'I am the Prefect and the Supreme One'. The ancient Vedic Rishis experienced this very Truth in the days of yore; and with an open heart, they vested this heritage to the human race.

Even today, to our utter astonishment and bewilderment, we find the very same heritage winding its course in every human heart to burst out like a midday sun to illuminate the globe and to shower the world of bliss over the human race by uniting them into 'one and oneness'. Through personal experiences as well as by bearing the proof of the 'oneness', it passes unchallenged, as it is experienced by the person himself. By these personal experiences, the challenger becomes a witness to the veracity of the Vedic Truth, nay, not an idle witness, but becomes an active announcer.

No, it is not confined here. Svetasvetar Upanishad announces, 'Let a man attain this Brahmahood (Supreme one) and in the immediate succession follows the Vedic Truth; that is, thousands and thousands of people will see him (the attainer of the Brahmahood) in his living human form, that is, the very identical form of the attainer within them and speak out the wonderful statement of the Vedic Truth.

The Vedic Truth is meant for the whole human race. It is not confined to any 'ism'. It is the cosmic law of mankind which conducts him in each and every second of his life; nay, it is the very vibration and the breathing of his heart. It evinces that the Vedas are not the monopoly of the Hindus alone; and again, it is not confined to any race and in India alone. It is meant for the lowliest of the low and the highest of the high. It pervades the globe from one end to the other.

And now, how this most wonderful miracle takes place in a man is related.

The Vedic lore runs thus:

'And thus this Man, rising from the lower plane to the seventh plane attains the Supreme Light and by his own form made of God's light, appears within myriads of people to prove his attainment of Brahmahood as he is the perfect and the Supreme One'.

"The attainer himself will also see almost all within himself whosoever will come in contact with him as has been mentioned in Kaivalya Upanishad, 'The attainer of Brahmahood will be seen by all in them (in their own bodies) and he himself will see all in him (i.e., within his own body) and there is nothing furthermore. This is 'One is All and All is One' – Pantheism.

This is the most mysterious feature of the miracle as it is nothing but the most unsurmountable miracle for one Man to be seen by myriads of men as long as he lives.

Now the question of solving the mystery and bringing out its nature in the daylight is left to the scientists.

WHAT IS ATMA OR SELF – DESCRIPTION OF VISUALIZING ATMA BY JIBANKRISHNA– ITS EFFECT

Jibankrishna narrated different stages of his visualizing Atma on different dates.

On March 11, 1956, He said, 'In the spiritual world visualizing 'Atma' or 'Soul' is fundamental. Who will have austerity he must have the visualization of Atma. And in one era only one must have this visualization, just like Sri Ramkrishna in his era. But this is not the end. There is no end to austerity. After visualizing Atma if He wishes He performs austerity within the seer's body. Then comes the austerity of Vedanta'.

On March 11, 1956, Diamond said, 'There is a specific age when this visualization of Atma occurs. I came to know by the grace of Sri Ramkrishna. It happens between twenty-four and twenty-five years of age. Sri Ramkrishna visualized

Atma at twenty-two – twenty-three years age and in my case, it was twenty-four years eight months age.

If at this age it occurs then it is all right, otherwise, it does not occur accurately'.

On December 21, 1961, Diamond said, 'What is Atma or Soul?' The whole life force of the human body including all the attributes percolates within the seventh plane, merged within Atma in finer form and visualize Atma from within Atma.'

One day in October 1956, Diamond narrated his experience while visualizing Atma, 'visualization of Atma occurs in lying condition when the body remains completely at rest. After visualization when my consciousness comes back, I saw myself in a lying condition. I couldn't say how long I was at this stage. After a long time, I got up.'

On February 6, 1956, Diamond said about the path from the sixth plane to the seventh plane for visualizing Atma, 'See there is a channel on the right side from the sixth plane to the seventh plane. When the seer's mind goes through this channel to the cerebrum Atma can be seen.

It is nobody's job to find out this mystery unless one has the visualization of Atma in full-fledged form.'

On June 27, 1961, Diamond described his experience in visualizing Atma, 'See, during this period, nothing can be said whether Kundalini or life force is moving upwards. The scene opens like this – Sri Ramkrishna extending his fingers and showing me Atma is saying – This is God, this is seeing of God. And I am seeing this from inside the Atma. Do you know what I was seeing? An aurora and within this, there is a thumb-like place demarcated by a fine blue lining. And inside that place, I am seeing a point, and encircling that point some atom-type particles are whirling. Next, that aura turned in the backside taking the shape of the tail of a comet. At that time it can be understood that something is moving through the organ of generation, the organ of evacuation, naval, heart, and throat and ultimately through the eyebrows enters the cerebrum (in between the middle and backside of the brain) and at that moment it ignites all on a sudden. But it does not take so much time as I am speaking. This happens long after visualizing Atma what happens? The passage becomes clear though during visualizing God the passage becomes clear to some extent. But this happens to clear the passage more distinctly. It cannot be understood then and there. I have understood it after a long time. Now, what is this individualistic austerity?

This has been mentioned in Upanishad though not so distinctly. But when you are seeing me in dreams is it within Upanishad? No! They have correctly mentioned about me when are saying, 'Thou art woman, thou art man, Thou art the youth and the maiden too; Thou as an old man tottering with a staff; Being born, thou becomest facing in every direction.'

[Svetasvetara Upanishad 4.3]. Vedic Rishis (Sages) could not mention you. What you have achieved is beyond Upanishad – a completely new phenomenon.

[What Jibankrishna has experienced in visualizing Atma or Soul has been mentioned in Katha Upanishad though not in such details.

It is mentioned as such:

"A person of the measures of a thumb in the inner soul; Ever seated in the heart of creatures; He is framed by the heart by the thought by the mind; They who know that, become immortal". (Svetasvetara Upanishad – 3.13)

Again Brihad-Aranyaka Upanishad has mentioned thus: This Person (Purusha) here in the heart is made of mind, is of the nature of light, is like a little grain of rice, is a grain of barley. This very one is the ruler of everything, is lord of everything, governs this whole universe, whatsoever there is. (5.5.6)

BRAHMAHOOD OR SUPREME STATE OF JIBANKRISHNA

On 1.6.1958 Diamond says:

The Brahma or Supreme Being of Sankaracharyya in one sense is a judicial word and what has been mentioned in Astabakra Sanghita about Brahma is very interesting. They are saying, 'Though Brahma is confined in a fixed place, all His actions are performed everywhere.' See, I am a man. Encircling me what an amazing incident is happening, but I am confined in my own dwelling place! From different places, you are coming to me and narrating your experiences. See what a wonderful quote Asrtabakra is giving! How it is tallying with our phenomenon! Sankar's 'Supreme Cult' is individualistic. And Samadhi state is a kind of death. What is its utility? Now I have crossed the region of Samadhi. I am a living human being, and this form is within everybody. This is termed as the state of full liberation in life. In an ascent state of austerity, we find the individualistic Supreme Cult confined within its own Self.

But in universalism in the state of descent how amazingly I am being manifested in so many people!

Lastly, I say that Astabakra is also saying, 'I bow to myself.' What a wonderful quote! Brahma or the Supreme Being is a living human being. He is confined in a place and he is enveloped throughout the world.

[Svetasvatar Upanishad has described such a person like this:

"The one God, hidden in all things; All-pervading, the Inner Soul of all beings; The overseer of deeds, in all things, abiding; The witness, the sole thinker, devoid of qualities". (6.11)

JIBANKRISHNA IS MERGED IN THE FIVE ELEMENTS AND FOR THIS REASON, HE APPEARS WITHIN THE HUMAN RACE

Rishi Uddalak said, 'I am Brahma', and now the human race is announcing that with me. Herewith is proof they are establishing these words. Listen, his phenomenon is the reconciliation of 'Advaitabad' and 'Visistadwaitabad. Some three thousand and five hundred years have rolled by. After so many years it has been proved here. Big incidents always happen in such a manner. For about eighteen years I have been continuing it and now I have conceived this matter and the world is carrying this proof to me.

I have become the life of the world. Can you say what is the requirement for this? To achieve such a state one should be merged into the five elements of nature. And I have become so when at my 13 years 8 months age Rajyoga was manifested within my body.

[Svetasvetara Upanishad has mentioned this all-pervading state as such:

"The Soul (Atman), which pervades all things,
As butter is contained in the cream,
Which is rooted in self-knowledge and austerity –
This is Brahma, the highest mystic doctrine!
This is Brahma, the highest mystic doctrine!". (1.16)

This has also reference in Chandyogya Upanishad about Universal man or Universal Soul as such:

Universal man – "who exists in varieties of human beings in his own form. And he exists in the form of earth, water, fire, wind, and sky."]

We have witnessed how the effect of the transformation into Universal man through five sheaths occurred in Jibankrishna.

Svetasvatara Upanishad has mentioned:

"When the fivefold quality of Yoga has been produced,
Arising from the earth, water, fire, air, and space,
No sickness, no old age, no death has he,
Who has obtained a body made out of the Fire of Yoga?" 2.12)

Jibankrishna explained on the basis of his achievement of this quality: Now we will see, how this Oneness is spread among human beings. The spiritual life of Diamond attaining Godhood gets itself thoroughly pervaded with the five elements of nature. The five elements are:-

(1) Sky or ether or atom- an invisible one; (2) Air; (3) Fire; (4) Water; (5) Earth.

These five elements of nature having the spirit of the very identical one, the attainer of the Godhood will function and carry the human form of attainer and place within the bodies of myriads of people and thus making one with Him in the spiritual world and thus oneness is established.

1) The function of the sky or ether or atom will bear its own proof. Some numberless people will see Him previously or hear His name.

2) Air functions in this way- Some people will hear His name and they see Him. It may run so far that you are

present here, hear His name and some of you may see Him and He shall make you known with particulars about Him.

3) The third element is fire, that is the eye. The eye represents the fire that is light and forces both combined. Let you come in contact with Him and you may see Him within.

4) Then comes water. There at the outset in the vital sheath bluish gurgling water is seen and the water, undergoing a numberless chemical and physical changes within the laboratory of the human body assumes the form of the sun in the cerebrum and the attainer of Godhood will be seen there in the sun.

5) Earth is the last of the elements and it also plays the most important role from one hemisphere to another hemisphere like this-

It has been observed in countless people when they read the book written by Diamond based on His personal spiritual experiences of the Vedic Truth within His body, they have seen Him within them. Why? Keep a book under the ground for a few months and the book will be transformed into earth.

Thus we find the five elements become the distributors of Oneness. A man by nature's selection becomes One or God

and this Godhood or Oneness is distributed through the agency of five elements and it is made a free gift because it is a free gift to Him by nature and so to humanity, making them One or God with Him and thereby it proves and evinces that each and every member of the human race is but God or One in the spiritual world. This is Universal One and Oneness.

[Svetasvetara Upanishad again mentions:

'He by whom this whole world is constantly enveloped,

Is intelligent, the author of time, possessor of qualities, omniscient.

Ruled over by Him work revolves –

This, which is regarded as earth, water, fire, air, and space". (6.2)]

THE MEANING OF BRAHMAJNAN OR SUPREME CULT

June 1958.

One day Jibankrishna said:

What is the meaning of 'Brahmajnan'or Supreme Cult? All become One. Nobody knows this meaning even today. Why so many diversions in the world? Due to lack of this oneness. Why so many diversions among Hindus, Muslims, Christians? It is due to a lack of oneness. Nothing will be there. There will be no necessity for temples, churches, mosques. When a man gets God within his own body it will then become a temple, church, mosque, etc. All will be extirpated automatically.

[Maitri Upanishad has mentioned about such a person thus:

"When a seer sees the brilliant
Maker, Lord, Person the Brahma-Source;
Then, being a knower, shaking off good and evil,
He reduces everything to unity in the Supreme Imperishable". (6.18)

POSSIBILITY OF THE ESTABLISHMENT OF 'ONENESS' IN THE FUTURE AMONG THE HUMAN RACE

23rd July 1958.

Thakur (Sri Ramkrishna) said, 'Man can never be a preacher or religious teacher.' What happened? He eradicated this theory and said, 'only God can be a religious teacher.' What did he do? He established God within the temple of the human body. Traditional religion cannot be universal. And if it is not universal, how the human race can achieve oneness?

You look at the world's religious history. What the incarnations are trying? They are trying to unite the human race. Now, look at Sri Ramkrishna. He said, 'The only object of human life is to achieve God' and then said, 'There are so many idealisms,, and so many ways.'

Now come to world history. What happened with the French revolution? Their slogan was, Liberty – Equality – Fraternity – trying to unite everybody. Karl. Marx tried to unite the human race through economic revolution and its indirect effect was seen in the Russian revolution in 1917. This is also an effort to unite the human race. But was it successful?

After so many days we are seeing a possibility of unification among mankind. Vedas have mentioned: There exists 'one' but others say, 'many'.

Now this 'many' will be 'one', though how much time it will take is very difficult to say. But we can say that this has started.

[Maitri Upanishad has mentioned thus:

"Verily, that One became threefold. He developed forth eightfold, elevenfold, twelvefold, into an infinite number of parts. Because of having developed forth, He is the created Being has entered into and moves among created beings; He became the overlord of created beings. That is the Soul (Atman) within and without – yea, within and without"! (5.2)

BRAHMA OR THE SUPREME SELF IS A LIVING HUMAN BEING

October-November, 1958

The natural motion of a human being is to be 'one' with each other. There is no difference between any caste, religion, gender, and age in the spiritual world. Listen, even if I have the least flaw, whatever has happened here, will be stopped. And I have no credit for all these. God is protecting us.

Sri Ramkrishna said, 'This world is not true. How this can be! Where will you see God? In this world, Brahma or the Supreme Being is the content and the world is the container. So the world and Brahma are both true. So, what we are getting finally? Brahma is in the form of a living person who is seen both outside and inside. And here the question of immortality comes. There is a quote in Rabindranath Tagore, 'After one hundred years from today.....'. So, if I live for one hundred years, I can see what will happen.

[In Brihad Aranyaka Upanishad a progressive attempt was made to conceive of Brahma. It was admitted that Brahma was to be found not only in the not-Self but also in the Self;

that it was not only the essence of the cosmical phenomenon but also of the organic and mental functions of the human person.

This probably was an outgrowth of the macrocosmic conception of an enormous human person. We find in Brihad-Aranyaka Upanishad where the great Sage Gargya said to king Ajatsatru of Benaras about Brahma thus:

The Person who is yonder in the sun – him indeed, I worship as Brahma!

The Person who is yonder in the moon – him, indeed, I worship as Brahma!

The Person who is here in fire – him, indeed, I worship as Brahma!

The Person who is here in a mirror – him, indeed, I worship as Brahma!

The Person here, who is in the body (Atman) – him, indeed, I worship as God!" [2.1]

On 1.2.1959 Diamond said :

Dr. Urquhart comments in Pantheism – 'The moral life thus becomes Universal to live in perfect goodness is to realize oneself in the All'. – A man, who is in perfect goodness, he feels himself within all. But where is the proof that he feels himself in all? But when the world will bear the proof that we are seeing you within ourselves? What will they say? You know that my body is the Abstract form of Soul (Atman) and you see, the same thing has been mentioned by a foreign philosopher David Hawkins in his book – In the Aristotelian tradition, the soul is described as the form of the body and by 'Form' is meant all the habitudes and capacities of that body.

……….. What I say frequently to you that as soon as you see me within yourselves, at that very moment you have achieved all aspects of my spiritualism though in the embryo. And it will expose itself according to the situation.

[Quotations from 'THE LANGUAGE OF NATURE' :
An essay in the philosophy of Science by David Hawkins (University of Colorado)
Publisher: W. H. Freeman & Co.
Sanfrancisco and London.

1."The learning is not in the life of the individual but in the transition to a new species. The individual, like the soul in Plato's account of it, may know but does not learn. If the species learns it does so only by becoming a new species." (Page 171 – Line 23)

2. "In the Aristotelian tradition the soul is described as the form of the body, and by 'form' is meant all the habitudes and capacities of the body." (Page 274 – Line 9)

On the above two quotations, Jibankrishna gave his interpretations on August 4, 1967.

1. As per Plato's version those who saw Jibankrishna within them they have achieved a new life, which means a new human race is created.

2. As per Aristotle's tradition the form of soul is the form of Jibankrishna which all of us see within us and the ultimate effect of such visualization is that we get the attributes and capacities of Jibankrishna.]

RELIGION IS NOT IMAGINATION, IT OCCURS IN THE FORM OF A HUMAN BEING

October-November, 1958

Diamond said one day, "This great conflict about in-form and formless God is a great mistake and imaginary. Imaginations are of three types:

1) Personal, when a man imagines many things;

2) Hereditary when this is running through heredity; and

3) Universal. There is a universal sketch of imagination that is expressed whenever it finds the opportunity.

The explanations mentioned in my books ('Dharma-O-Anubhuti' in Bengali and 'Religion and Realization' in English) are all based on my personal experiences. And those experiences are so deep that I cannot express. Even I am saying that those experiences are wrong, imaginary. Am I mad? Am I insane? No, far off from it! Nobody has got such a rational brain as I have and for this reason, such a wonderful phenomenon is created here. Could I think fifteen years back that so many people would see me in dreams and other states? God showed that religion is not imaginary; it is with a living person.

[In Brihad Aranyaka Upanishad a progressive attempt was made to conceive of Brahma. It was admitted that Brahma was to be found not only in the not-Self but also in the Self; that it was not only the essence of Cosmical phenomena but also of the organic and mental functions of the human person.

This probably was an outgrowth of the macrocosmic conception of an enormous human person.

We find in Brihad Aranyaka Upanishad where the great Sage Gargya said to king Ajatsatru of Benaras about Brahma thus:-

"The Person who is yonder in the sun – him, indeed I worship as Brahma!!
The Person who is here in the fire, - him, indeed I worship as Brahma!
The Person who is here in a mirror, - him, indeed, I worship as Brahma!
The Person here, who is in the body (Atman), - him, indeed, I worship as God!" (2.1)
Again Katha Upanishad has mentioned the Person or Purusha in the highest course in such a way:
"Higher than the senses are the objects of sense,
Higher than the objects of senses is the mind;
And higher than the mind is the intellect.
Higher than the intellect is the Great Self (Atman).
Higher than the Great is the Unmanifest (avyakta),
Higher than the Unmanifest is the Person.
Higher than the Person there is nothing at all.
That is the goal. That is the highest course". (3.10-11)]

GOD IS NOWHERE ELSE EXCEPT THIS HUMAN BODY

March 3, 1959.

Sri Ramkrishna says, 'I shall see, Lord Hari (a name of God in Hindu scripture) everywhere in this universe'. The esoteric meaning is that when the mind reaches the fourth plane wherever the eyesight falls only the light is seen. This refers to the sayings of Thakur (Sri Ramkrishna), 'Is it yellow fever that everywhere I am seeing you'! But what is this 'you'? Even Srimad Bhagavat Gita is saying, 'wherever the eyesight falls, I am seeing Lord Krishna'. But where is the proof that he is seeing Krishna? Now come here! I am appearing within the human bodies and they are seeing me, and when they are bearing this proof, this universe enveloped with God' comes true from both sides. A living man sees him within himself and he also sees innumerable human beings within himself. This is mentioned in Kashmir Shaivism'- 'Iswartatva' and 'Sadvidya'. 'One is all and all is one' – Pantheism.

We are now witnessing this great 'Truth' in our own eyes. But I am not only seeing you within myself, at the same time you are also seeing me within yourselves. This is the near proof of the term 'The universe is enveloped with God', otherwise, all are merely imagination. From time immemorial mankind has been seeking 'Truth', trying to feel 'Truth', trying to realize 'Truth', but the scholars and so-called saints and priests took undue advantage of the fervent mentality of the human race and misguided them.

They diverted the spontaneous evolution of the life power of the human body.

Where is God? Is he in a temple, mosque, or church? But with that idea, nothing was obtained. But look here! You are seeing me within yourselves and I am also seeing you within myself. Thus where is God and what is God – this confusion is eradicated forever.

[Katha Upanishad has mentioned:

1. The Inner Soul (Antaratma) of all things…

Who makes his one form manifold,

Is performing a piece of supernatural magic

In appearing as many. (5.12)

2. "The Self-existent pierced the openings (of the senses) outward;

Therefore one looks outward, not within himself.

Certain wise men, while seeking immortality,

Introspectively beheld the Soul (Atman) face to face". (4.10)]

VISUALIZING DIAMOND WITHIN THE BODY IS THE PRACTICAL RELIGION WHICH IS NOT MENTIONED IN THE VEDIC ERA

25.7.1959

The phenomenon happening here is neither knowledge nor devotion. Even if you say this as 'Religion', it is a practical Religion. We are corroborating this both from inside and outside. This is a continuous process. Many things I cannot tell you. Unless these manifest outside, how can I tell you! But still, you see, these have manifested in my practical life. So far this phenomenon has manifested outside, it is true in our life. Here the quote of the Rishis uttered thousands of years ago 'one exists' is flooded away. The Truth is 'one', and that was unknown to them, why? Then so many religions would not have come into this world.

[Mundaka Upanishad has mentioned about this person existing outside and inside thus:

"Heavenly, formless is the person (Purusha)
He is without and within, unborn,
Breathless, mindless, pure
Higher than the high Imperishable". (2.1.2)

WHEN A PERSON IS TRANSFORMED INTO SOUL OR ATMA WITH HIS FORM ITS PROOF IS BORNE BY MANKIND

26.7.59

The phenomenon of visualizing God or Atma (soul) does not carry much sense as it is very rare. Thousands of years ago Rishis announced, 'Atma can be seen.' Then thousands of years passed by, we find that Thakur (Sri Ramkrishna) had visualized God as he said, 'I swear that I have seen God'. But within these long years, there is no evidence that anybody saw God so specifically. So what have I told you? God has transformed me step by step. The proof of my transformation into a universal soul with my form is borne by myriads of people irrespective of caste and creed, religion, gender, and age. My own form is the form of the human soul: Esa Atmeti (I am the Soul – Upanishad).

The individualistic austerity (in the full-fledged form) will never occur because we have surpassed that stage and got universal austerity. And if anybody does not visualize Atma or Soul, what will remain? Man – you exist. But am I getting peace? Where is this peace? 'Sah Aham' – I am 'He'. But who is 'He'? He is Brahma (Supreme Self). But now come on. Have you seen that Brahma? Among four hundred billion people even if three to four persons see that 'Brahma', that is insignificant. Suppose mankind believes and obeys these persons. But what they have achieved? Nothing! So long this 'He' was unknown to mankind. But now we have the right to say, 'Yes, we have seen this 'He' and he is the form of a living human being and this is my form. So this 'He' is a human being and this is my form. So this 'He' is within our knowledge now. So far mankind believed three to four persons who had individual austerity as in the case of Thakur (Sri Ramkrishna) who said, 'I swear that I have visualized God' and the world believed his words. Even Swami Vivekananda revolted against such words and he said, 'In recent days people started talking such peculiar things, but it is quite to have such realizations in recent days. So one has to believe the religion'. Then he said, 'I don't believe it.' Now, he disbelieved, but what matters to this? But what I have told you? The spontaneous austerity which has happened within me never happened and will not happen with anyone in the future. On what ground people will believe this individual austerity? 'Belief is not religion' – I have mentioned it so many times and have written it in my book (Religion and Realization). So long the world was based on this 'Belief' and this term 'He' was also based on 'Belief'. But now we have got the proof.

Now it is not based on 'Belief' but on 'Evidence'.

[The proof of seeing Jibankrishna within the body in dreams, trances, meditation, and even in reality, was borne by myriads of people and is still borne even after his death in 1967.

Chandogya Upanishad has described such a phenomenon as such:

"And the Blessed man, rising from the lower physical plane (to the seventh plane) attains the Supreme Light, and in his own form made of God's light, appears within myriads of people to prove his attainment of the Supreme Light or the Brahmahood, as He is the Perfect and the Supreme One". (8.12.3)]

'HE IS ONE' AS MENTIONED BY VEDIC RISHIS IS JUDICIAL BUT DIAMOND'S ONENESS IS A PROOF

On 27.7.1959 Diamond says:

In his book 'Buddhism and Vedantism' Swami Vivekananda has mentioned in the synopsis with his great intellect in such a nice manner which nobody could do so far. He has mentioned – The Buddhists say – variety – this is Truth. This means mankind – individually without even taking into account his selfhood – Truth.

And Vedantists are saying – These varieties which you are seeing outside, are nothing. That is Maya (illusion) – short-lived apparent – merely shadow. Within you there exists 'one' and that is the 'Truth'. Now to us, this question arises – what is that 'one'? Nobody can answer. But what God is showing us? Within varieties there is oneness. And that oneness does not belong to the Vedantists in the form of imagination or judicial. This oneness comprises a living human being. It encircles my form and is established with proof forever. Among myriads of people, my form is manifested and they are announcing what is that one. We have no separate existence in the spiritual world. Only you exist, though outside we are different. This is the Truth that innumerable people have established. So the doctrine of the Buddhists, 'The varieties are Truth' and the Vedantists' imaginary 'one' does not exist.

[Katha Upanishad is saying:

"The Inner Soul (Antaratma) of all things,
Who makes his own form manyfold,
Is performing a piece of supernatural magic
In appearing as many". (5.12)

WHAT IS THE AUSTERITY OF FIVE SHEATHS – ITS EFFECT

August 1959.

Evolution and Revelation – what is Evolution? Visualization of God occurs – what is that? Both Evolution and Revelation both.

At first, I saw water in Pranamaya Kosha (Sheath) comprising three planes: an organ of generation, an organ of evacuation and naval region) – What happens? Evolved. In Manomaya Kosha (Sheath comprising of fourth plane or heart). That water is transformed into God's light – Evolved. In Vijnanamaya Kosha (Sheath comprising of the fifth plane, the sixth plane and portion of the seventh plane) when the mind comes to the fifth plane or the throat. I saw the sky – what happens? Evolved. Then again in Vijnanamaya Kosha when the mind comes to the sixth plane (middle of the two eyebrows on the forehead) I saw the knowledge of the eye and within it the image of Buddha in meditation. When the mind comes to the seventh plane (AnandamayaKosha (Sheath of Bliss where the man is transformed into Bliss)

After these stages in the descent, I visualized the divine consciousness in the cerebrum which descended up to the region of the waist and lastly, I saw the manikin form of God and was transformed into God – everything is evolution.

After all these evolutionary processes the seer is transformed into the soul of every human being and becomes universal – this is also evolution – Man is born so. So what is the natural motion of a human being? He has come to this world to become God. For example, in the materialistic world diamond and carbon. What is the scientific definition of Diamond? A superior form of carbon. So what is a human body? It is a coal mine. What is happening then? Diamond is prepared. That is God. This body is transformed into God.

[Mundaka Upanishad has described such person as a macrocosmic person and says:

"Fire is his head; His eyes, the moon, and sun;

The regions of space, His ears; His voice, the revealed Vedas;

Wind, His breath (Prana0; His heart, the whole world;

Out of His feet, The earth. Truly, He is the Inner Soul (Atman) of all". (2.1.4)

FOR THE ACHIEVEMENT OF GOD, NO MONK LIFE IS REQUIRED

August 1959.

Ramanuj discarded the Sannyasi (Monk) Institution of Sankaracharya. He never left his monastery. But what type of monk was he! Do you know what are the strictures of a monk's life? They will never stay anywhere for more than three days, even will not stay more than a night under a tree.

Now come to Thakur (Sri Ramkrishna). He taught us all that there is no need for monk life. He used to wear dhoti, with a sandal on his feet, a coat on his body, and a monkey cap on his head. On one side he was a Paramhansa (the highest state of spiritualism according to Vedanta).

Then come here. What is the further development? See, nothing is required. I don't know a single mantra (hymn), I never worshipped any Gods and Goddesses with a single flower.

Remember, with all shortcomings a man is Brahma (God) – there is no barrier to check it.

Mundaka Upanishad has mentioned thus:

"This Soul (Atman) is not to be obtained by instruction,
Nor by the intellect, nor by much learning.
He is to be obtained only by the one whom He chooses;
To such a one that Soul (Atman) reveals His own person". (3.2.3)

About outside signs, again Mundaka Upanishad has mentioned:

"(Soul or Atma cannot be obtainable) Not by sign is it grasped, not even by speech,

Not by any other sense-organs, austerity or work". (3.2.8)]

SUPREME CULT IS TO BE ACHIEVED WITHIN THIS LIFE

August 1959.

Nachiketa went to Yama (god of death) to know the mystery of death (Katha Upanishad), which means to know what was after death. They did not want to see this life. They did not know how wonderful this life was. What do I say to you? This human life is all. Whatever will be done will take place in this present life, otherwise, there is nothing after death. Whatever you can do, do it within this present life.

What do I say? I want to live with this physical body forever. Those who have achieved this truth, don't know what is death, even they don't think about death.

See this body! What a wonderful thing has happened! They didn't want to know what was light, on the contrary, searched for what was in the dark.

Listen, I am not a Hindu, not a Muslim, not a Christian. I am only a man who is Jibankrishna. Nothing is there within me except me – I am the measure.

Keno Upanishad has mentioned:

"When known by an awakening, It [Brahma or Supreme Self] is conceived of;
Truly it is immortality one finds.
With the Soul (Atman) one finds power;
With knowledge, one finds the immortal". (2.12.4)
'If one has known [It] here (in this life), then there is Truth.
If one has known [It] not here, great is the destruction.
Discerning [It] in every single being, the wise,
On departing from this world, becomes immortal". (2.13.5)

I AM ONE AND MANY

December 5, 1959

Swami Vivekananda has mentioned, '.... then alone he has reached the universal brotherhood and that man alone is Vedantist.' But the term 'Brotherhood' does not stand. In another place, he is saying, '.... Therefore Vedanta formulates not universal brotherhood but universal oneness' (complete works Volume -VIII). Big exploitation of a big personality! Which one will be taken by human beings? Whether universal brotherhood or Universal Oneness?

But what we are seeing here? I am seeing myself with the eye of the whole human race. I am one and at the same time, I am many. His is that version of the great Vedic Rishis, 'you are born to become Universal.'

BrihadAranyaka Upanishad has mentioned thus:

"He became corresponding in form to every form.

This is to be looked upon as a form of him.

Indra (Brahma) by his magic powers (Maya) goes about in many forms;

Yoked is his ten-hundred steeds.

He (i.e., the Soul or Atman), verily, is the steeds.

He, verily, is tens and thousands, many and endless.

This Brahma is without an earlier and without a later,

Without an inside and without an outside.

This Soul is the Brahma, the all-perceiving. – Such is the instruction". (2.5.19)

JIBANKRISHNA - BEYOND ALL ATTRIBUTES AND TIME

17.1.1960

What is the attribute of God? He is 'one'. So whenever anybody sees me within them, they are getting my attribute or they are becoming 'one'. And what is the meaning of 'beyond all attributes'? See, Bhola, his father, his son; Jiten, his father, his son – all see me in dreams, meditation, and trances. It means a boy's 'satva', young one's 'rajas' and old man's 'tamo' (creation, existence, and destruction), with all these attributes they are seeing me within them. So I am not only beyond these three attributes but beyond time. See, that Brahma is beyond these three attributes – such proof has not been cited so distinctly by anyone so long. So you are very fortunate that seeing my form within you, you are also being beyond these three attributes. To understand such a phenomenon will take some time which you cannot realize now. In the long run, you will realize it with proof.

[Svetasvatara Upanishad has mentioned thus –

"The One God, hidden in all things; All-pervading, the Inner Soul of all things; The overseer of deeds(Karman), in all things abiding; the witness, the sole thinker, devoid of qualities (Nirguna)".

THE REAL MEANING OF 'SHIVA' – THE GOODNESS – 'HE IS ONE' AS MENTIONED IN UPANISHADS – THE FORM OF JIBANKRISHNA

On 1.2.1960 Diamond said -

What is this form of 'Shiva – goodness'? You cannot conceive anything through the past. Those words are personified here. Shiva – the goodness' has been used as an adjective of 'Shiva – the oneness'. Atharva Veda has mentioned, 'He is one'. Then he becomes Truth. Now, come on and say, Who is this Shiva – the goodness? Listen, my form is the form of Shiva – the goodness. Why do Hindus see me, Muslims see me, Christians see me, Jews see me within themselves? In one word, who appears among myriads of people irrespective of religions, castes, ages, and sexes is the real Shiva – the goodness. How many times I have told you, don't take the abstract idea of religion. When you see the proof, then only you should take it.

[Svetasvatara Upanishad has mentioned:

"Thou art woman. Thou art man.

Thou art the youth and the maiden too.

Thou as an old man tottering with a staff.

Being born, Thou becomest facing in every direction". (4.3)

Again in Svetasvetara Upanishad, it is mentioned:

Who is the face, the head, the neck of all,

Who dwells in the heart all things,

All-pervading is He, and bountiful,

Therefore omnipotent and kindly (Siva)". (3.11)]

OUTSIDE JIBANKRISHNA IS GOD - INSIDE HE IS THE OWN SELF OF HUMAN BEING

Maitri Upanishad says:

"Verily, that one became threefold. He developed forth fold, eightfold, elevenfold, twelvefold, into an infinite number of parts. Because of having developed forth, He is the created being, has entered into and moves among created beings. That is the Soul (Atman) within and without – yea, within and without"! (5.2)

How this has manifested in Jibankrishna or Diamond will be revealed through his discussion:

One day in February 1960 Jibankrishna discussed:

Visualization of God is not so much high ranking in the spiritual world. That may be compared with the matriculation examination (Final year of school examination). What innumerable realizations I got in my life cannot be expressed. For this reason, sometimes I think about how have I survived! One thing I should tell you and try to keep in your memory. When you will see me outside I am becoming God and when you will see me within the body, I become your own self.

Each and every human being is controlling this world. Each animal and other creatures are controlling this world. Each tree is controlling the world. Whoever has a reaction is controlling the world. See those cow dung pallets on the wall! These are also controlling the world. How? By spreading the obnoxious odor in the surroundings they are controlling the world. So, what is the sum total? The world is controlled spontaneously.

I am not a Hindu in a true sense. I am without any race or religion. In a dream once I said to myself that I have no race or religion.

Whenever you have seen me within you, mind that you become without any race or religion.

RE-ESTABLISHMENT OF BRAHMAVIDYA OR SUPREME CULT THROUGH JIBANKRISHNA

On 30.4.1960 Diamond said -

Listen, this phenomenon (manifestation of the supreme cult) has happened in our country a long time before. Now we are trying to explain it by our worldly consciousness. This is a mysterious phenomenon that has happened here and it is beyond any explanation.

'I was one and have become many' – we have got specific proof of this here. In Upanishads they have mentioned it like this, 'In the beginning, there was self alone in the shape of a person';" your soul is the inner self of all beings!' 'All is one' – when all of you see me within yourselves. This universe is within every human being. Everybody is projecting this world from within him and visualizes. I am within you and you are within me. It is very difficult to conceive it due to Maya (Illusion) or the worldly attributes of the body. When one dies, the world vanishes to him but remains as such to others. And another thing I use to mention frequently is that past, present, and future, everything is within a human body. And here no question of rebirth or previous birth arises. According to Swami Vivekananda, 'When the knowledge of self is manifested, it is realized that there is no rebirth. Otherwise, everything is there.'

I have become all these. In Vedas there is only one adjective with God – 'He is one' and this we are witnessing here. I am placing a challenge that no desire can exist beyond this oneness within a human being and nothing exists after it.

[Svetasvatara Upanishad has mentioned;

"The past, the future, and what the Vedas declare –

This whole world the illusion maker projects

Out of this". (4.9)

JIBANKRISHNA IS BEYOND ANY KNOWLEDGE

11.7.1960

Do I ask you one question? Who am I? Why do you see me both outside and inside? I am a man. But why do people see me within themselves? You are also a man. Do you know what kind of man I am? I am such a person about whom nothing can be known. You have plenty of realizations, you are Brahmavid (Person who has known Brahma or Supreme Being). But this is not the end of this phenomenon. You will see me the next night, then again, and so on. And not only you, people irrespective of religion, gender, and age are seeing me in dreams, etc. There is no end to it. And at last, you will say, 'Alas! We have come to know nothing'!

[Svetasvetar Upanishad has mentioned about such person thus:

'Without foot or hand, he is swift and a seizer! He sees without eye; He hears without ear! He knows whatever is to be known; Him there is none who knows. Men call Him the Great Primeval Person". (3.1)

GOD SHOULD BE ACHIEVED WITHIN THIS LIFE

July 14, 1960.

In the Gospel, Thakur Sri Ramkrishna was saying, 'Before dying one has to make austerity for achieving God.' Hearing this Jibankrishna said to the listeners, 'That means before dying one has to achieve Godhood; But how many days before he should achieve? Is it ten minutes before dying? No, my boy! It starts from the age of 12 years 4 months and so long he will live, this austerity continues. And what Thakur has said is, 'The main object of human life is to achieve God, and that should be achieved before dying. But what has happened in our case? Oh, how fortunate we are, can you say! In our case, we achieve Godhood beforehand whatever an old man comes here, and what is about coming here? So many people have seen me before and then have come here. Hegel is saying, 'God is going to realize Himself through the manifestation of the universe.' This is partly true. He had no idea that the seed as well as this universe, are the same. This is a realization of Vedanta and he had not this experience. So how could he know this! Go above this and you will know that this universe is merely a sound. Again there is something beyond it. By reaching there everything becomes silent.

Keno Upanishad has mentioned:

"When known by an awakening, It [Brahma or Supreme Self] is conceived of;

Truly it is immortality one finds.

With the Soul (Atman) one finds power;

With knowledge, one finds the immortal". (2.12.4)

'If one has known [It] here (in this life), then there is Truth.

If one has known [It] not here, great is the destruction.

Discerning [It] in every single being, the wise,

On departing from this world, becomes immortal". (2.13.5)

BRAHMA REMAINS ACTIVE EVEN IN AN INERT STATE WHICH IS ESTABLISHED IN JIBANKRISHNA'S LIFE

24.9.1960

Upanishad is mentioning, 'Who is Brahma or Supreme Being, never goes anywhere to make propaganda that He is Brahma'. But nowhere proof is mentioned. Can you give its proof? To see my form within you is its proof. The best proof is, who, without seeing, hearing, or knowing about me' has seen my form within them. When a man is transformed into Supreme Being, he need not say, 'I have seen God'. The human race will say, "Thou art woman, thou art man; Thou art the youth and the maiden too; Thou as an old man tottering with a staff, Being born, Thou becomest facing in every direction". (Svetasvatara Upanishad 4.3)

A FORECAST BY JIBANKRISHNA ABOUT ACHIEVING THE CONTROLLING POWER IN THE SPIRITUAL WORLD

October 13, 1960.

Swamiji (Swami Vivekananda) says, 'All the religions of the world are but a hypothesis.' But see what has happened here! Don't take it as religion, I don't consider it as religion. Nothing is there except seeing my form within the body. You are seeing a living man within your body and thus far, nothing else. My boys what should I say! You have got this human life and how wonderful it is I cannot explain. I have understood what immense power this human brain has got. See this life power! What infinite power it has got! Just see, without my knowledge, this life power has spread throughout the world. And where is the proof? It is my form. This is proof that you see my form within your body.

Again see, the life power which has spread throughout the world has again centralized within my body. The world which is outside, at the same time is within me. It is absurd that the human race will see my form within them and narrate to me, and I have understood this. So I have centralized the whole world within me. What will happen due to this? Whatever will arise in the mind will manifest within the human race, by which this sense of oneness will spread among them and unite all into one, but this will happen without their knowledge. Of course, this may happen if it manifests. Let us wait and see.

Svetasvatara Upanishad has mentioned this person as a man with super human powers thus:

"Who is the face, the head, the neck of all,
Who dwells in the heart of all beings,
All-pervading is He, and bountiful;
Therefore omnipotent and kindly (Siva)". (3.11)

ONENESS IS MANIFESTED IN JIBANKRISHNA

26.10.1960

What is the knowledge of oneness? A man sees that he only remains on earth. Then coming down he sees this world and the existence of many. When this 'many' will come and tell you, "These 'many' which you are seeing outside are you". Then the real sense of 'Oneness' will grow within you. This whole phenomenon is for all human beings. Upanishad has mentioned about 'Man' only. Now you say, 'why all of you are seeing my form within you? I am an ordinary man. Isn't so? So what does it prove? These things are only for human beings. The body of a human being carries the power of infinity which cannot be fathomed. How wonderful it is!

[Katha Upanishad has mentioned:

"Him who is the constant among the inconstant,
The Intelligent among intelligencies,
The One among many, who grants desires –
The wise who perceive Him as standing in oneself,
They, and no others, have eternal peace"! (5.13)

THE SPIRITUAL ONENESS IS MANIFESTED AUTOMATICALLY

19.12.1960.

Listen, whenever there is a necessity for a new thing in the world, then and there it will happen automatically. This means this new thing is created within the human body automatically, and then this whole mankind gets that thing automatically within their bodies. Now you say, what is that new thing?

The eternal question comes humanity – who am I and what is my relationship with humanity. What impractical and imaginary thoughts are being impressed on manikin! Now, you see how God has solved this query with scientific proof. I am a living human being – just like you, but the human race is one with me. My form is manifested within the human body and they have announced:

"Thou art woman. Thou art man. Thou art the youth and the maiden too. Thou as an old man tottering with a staff. Being born, thou becomest facing in every direction." [Svetasvatara Upanishad – 4.3]

They have assumed this 'you' as 'one Atma' within all. But how is that 'Soul' (Atma)? Then they will remain silent and there is an excuse to suppress that question – 'He is beyond and any conception and mind'. Then you can't say anything. So Swami Vivekananda has announced Atma (or Soul) as a doctrine. No! This universal oneness is that new thing that is manifested here. Besides this, there are innumerable new things that may manifest in the future.

THE PERSON IN BRAHMAPURA (CEREBRUM) IS A LIVING HUMAN BEING JIBANKRISHNA AND SEEING HIM WITHIN THE BODY, RELIGION STARTS

23.12.1960

Seeing of God-the-Preceptor within the body occurs at the age of 12 years 4 months age though that realization is individualistic.

Then when the real religion starts and where? According to Vedas, one must see that Purusha of the Cerebrum or Brahmapur and then the religion starts. It is proved here that the person of Brahmapur is a living man, not imaginary or a supposed object. As soon as you are seeing me within your body 'oneness' is established. And the achievement of this 'oneness' is religion. Then when the religion starts? From my appearance within you, this is applicable to Hindus, Muslims, Christians, and the whole human race.

[Chandogya Upanishad has mentioned several thousands of years ago as such:

"And thus the Blessed man, rising from the lower physical plane (to the seventh plane)) attains the Supreme Light, and in his own form made of God's Light, appears within myriads of people to prove his attainment of the Supreme Light or the Brahmahood, as He is the Perfect and the Supreme One". (8.12.3)]

THE PROOF OF UPANISHAD'S VERSION 'YOU HAVE BECOME UNIVERSAL' IS FIRST BORNE BY A MAN IN THE PRESENT ERA

17.1.1961. 'Incarnation is the Semitic Religion', not Vedic cult. Now you see what has happened here? My image is being seen in every human being and then what lesson does it bear? A man says, 'See, you and I are one.' Outside we are many, but inside we are one in the form of a living man. This is the first time living proof that every human being is one inside. And that proof is not borne by me but you. I don't know anything about it unless you come and tell me. How wonderful! So long individual man said and the world listened, but here is vice-versa – the world is saying and one man listens with great astonishment –

"Thou art woman. Thou art man; Thou art the youth and the maiden too; Thou as an old man tottering with a staff; Being born, thou becomes facing in every direction". [Svetasvatara Upanishad 4.3]

TRUTH CANNOT BE ACHIEVED BY EXERTION – IT REVEALS SPONTANEOUSLY

19.1.1961.

Suka, Janak, Narada, are mythological personnel. Why were they created by Puran makers? Just to create an idealism. Now the question is, whether this idealism can give the Truth to human beings. Well, let me say that they created metaphors in a very simple manner. But what is the objective? Is it idealism and does it give the Truth? No! Never! Why? Oh! Truth is revealed spontaneously. Whenever an attempt will be taken to produce Truth through idealism this will become an exertion and exertion can never give Truth. This is clearly mentioned in Upanishads –

"(This Soul (Atma) is not to be obtained by instruction, Nor by the intellect, nor by much learning. He is to be obtained only by the one whom he chooses; To such one that Soul (Atman) reveals his own person". [Katha Upanishad 2.23]

THE FORM OF JIBANKRISHNA IS THE FORM OF ATMA OR SELF OF EVERY HUMAN BEING AND ITS PROOF

27.2.1961

Vedas say, 'Ekam Rupam Bahudha Yah Karoti' (One form becomes many). But where is that proof? Mankind has assumed that the same Atma or soul is within every human being. Swami Vivekananda has mentioned it as a hypothesis. But he is not correct. It can be visualized within the body. But so what? Among five hundred billion people, if one person visualizes Atma, that is not proof, though to an individual it is true. But in that issue think, what a clear conception of Upanishads has given! They are saying, 'Svena Rupena Abhinispadyate, (your form is transformed into the form of every human being) Sah Uttama Purusha' (He is the best man). And the form of this best man is the Atma or Self. But even they could not cite any proof which you are bearing now by seeing my form within you. Remember, I am a living human being.

[In Maitri Upanishad it is mentioned:

"Verily, that One became threefold. He developed forth eight-fold, eleven-fold, twelve-fold, into an infinite number of parts. Because of having developed forth, He is a created being, has entered into and moves among created beings; He became the overlord of created beings. That is the Soul (Atman) within and without – yea, within and without"! ((5.2)]

ACHIEVEMENT OF GODHOOD WITHIN JIBANKRISHNA HAPPENS BY SOME UNKNOWN FORCE

1.5.1961.

Rig-Veda said, 'He is one' (God is one) and Upanishads said, 'I am Brahma.' When Rishis could not find anything outside, they turned towards their own bodies and then uttered, 'I am Brahma.' Then comes 'questions about Brahma.' Though it would be correct had they say, ' questions about myself.' Now I have understood that this 'myself' is exposed here. Sri Ramkrishna said, ' Visualizing God,' 'Being God'. By his grace, I have achieved these two. But you see, my individualistic austerity and revelations are not the cause for these achievements. I had these experiences to understand the individualistic realizations. Some force is there which did all these within me, and I don't know anything about it. But it is true that all these have come through my body. There is no outside agency. But it is a strange thing that I don't know ' A, B, C' of it. Some unknown force has done it.

THE TRUTH IS THIS HUMAN BODY AND THE DIVINE CONSCIOUSNESS WHICH IS THE FORM OF JIBANKRISHNA

14.6.1961

So long only metaphors and symbols were the sum and substances of religions. But symbolism or metaphors are not the truth. Then what is the truth? This human body and the divine consciousness. Within that consciousness, there is a form and you have seen that, and in what stage? In dreams, and all these fellows in this room have seen my form. Now say, when the form of a man is manifested within myriads of people, what will you call it? Listen, in the embryo stage within the womb of a mother my form exists. And that proof is borne by children, boys, young and old ones, mothers whenever they are saying that they have seen my form within themselves. Now you can deny life power as you have not seen it, you can deny consciousness, but you cannot deny my form which is reality. I exist both on the outside and inside. Then you must admit that my form is real and guides this human body. This is the sum and substance. You can raise the question of whether this is true only for the present, and in my absence, this will be abolished? No! This form is eternal. [This is established by the fact when Katho Upanishad mentions:

"A Person of the measure of a thumb,
Like a light without smoke,
Lord of what has been and what is to be,
He alone is today, and tomorrow too'. (4.13)]

JIBANKRISHNA IS THE PURUSHA WHO AWAKES IN DREAMS AS MENTIONED IN UPANISHAD

It was 14th June 1961, Monday.

Diamond once said to the listeners present in his room at Kadamtala, Howrah in context to divine dreams, "See I should tell you one thing about divine drams. What is a dream? It relates to the Soul or Atman. Ney, it is not the Soul. Whenever I shall use the term 'Soul' some imaginary object will come into the brain. It is the spontaneous evolution of the life power of the human body. But I am talking about the divine dream, not the animal dream which is the expression of the subconscious state. It is not so with divine dreams. Even I should not term as 'Life'. Have you seen the form of 'Life'? No! You have seen my divine form within you. So my form is your life. Vedas have said, 'When will be the manifestation of this life power? When a man goes to sleep. Though this term 'dream' is not appropriate. Vedas have mentioned, 'within the dream, the person who awakes He is Brahma (supreme)'. And His different sportive forms you see within your dream. When this happens during ascent (progress towards Susupti) it may not be true. But when it comes down during descent from Susupti, it becomes true.

This has reference in Katha Upanishad (5.8) like this:
"Who fashions desire after desire, that indeed is the pure; That is Brahma; That indeed is called the Immortal; On it, all the worlds do rest; and no one soever goes beyond it"?
In this context, Diamond said, 'Without dream that Purusha (the Supreme Being mentioned in Vedas) won't awake. So within the dream, He awakes without any doubt and this waking state will spread in the future. Remember one thing always, that Purusha and Soul have become identical. So why should we call it Soul or Atman when nobody except one or two has visualized. But my own form which myriads of people have seen in various ways within them is not an imagination or perception. It is real and direct.

THE LIFE POWER OF HUMAN BEINGS IS THE FORM OF JIBANKRISHNA AND HIS SPORTIVE FORMS ARE SEEN IN DREAMS

19.6.1961

Let me say something about dreams. What is a dream? it is a sportive form of Atma or soul. No, let me not mention the term 'Atma' otherwise it may create some imaginary data about 'Atma'. The dream is the spontaneous manifestation of life power within a human body. But I am talking about only divine dreams, not animal dreams which are the expressions of the subconscious mind in a human body. But why should I mention life power? Have you seen life power? You are seeing my archetype form. So my form is your life power.

Vedas are saying: When this spontaneous manifestation will occur? When a man sleeps. It is not proper to call it a dream. Vedas are mentioning when a man sleeps this 'Purusha' (person of divine consciousness) appears and He is called 'Brahma' or the Supreme Being. And you see the various sportive forms of this Purusha when you sleep. When this revelation occurs in ascent (towards Susupti, i.e, after the stage of dream), the dream may or may not be true. But when the life force comes down from Susupti, the dream becomes true in all respects.

[Katha Upanishad has mentioned:

"He who is awake in those that sleep; The Person who fashions desire after desire – That indeed is the Pure. That is Brahma; That indeed is called the Immortal. On it all the world does rest; and no one soever goes beyond it". (5.8).

JIBANKRISHNA'S UNIVERSAL FORM IS ESTABLISHED

12.7.1961

From where my austerity in real form has started? First, in Pranamaya Kosha (sheath) I saw bluish gurgling water in my lower abdomen (in the 3rd plane). What I have seen in the fourth plane (Manomaya Kosha) – God's light. In the fifth plane, I have seen the sky (Marut) and in the cerebrum, I have seen the cosmic zone. And now at the age of 69 years, when the eyes are losing the power of sight, the ears are losing the power of hearing, the skin is becoming loose, I saw the foot (Earth). What does it mean? I have grown my control on Earth.

When I visualized water, light, sky, and cosmic zone it meant that after having my full control over these elements, these appeared in their own forms within my body teaching me that controlling power is established within me over these elements.

So many years have passed since I saw those elements, and now I have full control over the earth: That means I am the Master of these five elements.

When I saw the foot, did I wish to see it? Not as I saw it spontaneously, in the same way, I have acquired the controlling power over the five elements. This means the attributes of my body are such. This is termed in yoga as 'Bhutasiddha' (control over the five elements). Yes, it is showing the completion – the completion of universalism, oh! How the Rishis have termed it as 'Paravidya' (Supreme Cult). Otherwise, think that for no reason I saw my own foot! And this dream was manifested in my brain. See, if you are judicious on the basis of Vedas, then I shall say - 'completion'. Because they have mentioned that 20,000 won't do, it should be innumerable people to see a man attaining Godhood in dreams. Now, even more than that have seen me within them, and that is irrespective of caste, religion, gender, and age. Still, it has not stopped, on the contrary, it is increasing still I should say one thing to you – Even if a single person on earth is left to see me, then that flow is mine, not of mankind. Yet, keep it in mind, whether I live or die, this phenomenon of seeing me within the body will continue. I have come to know.

Taittiriya Upanishad has mentioned such a person having austerity through different sheaths. They have mentioned this man as a macrocosmic Person and mentioned as such: "Fire is His head; His eyes, the moon, and sun; the regions of space, His eyes; His voice, the revealed Vedas; Wind, His breath; His heart, the whole world. Out of His feet, the earth. Truly, He is the inner Soul (Atman) of all". (2.1.4).

WHEN A MAN BECOMES SUPREME BEING HE BECOMES ONE WITH THE HUMAN RACE

14.7.1961.

The Vedic Rishis are saying, 'I am Brahma' (Supreme Being). Then who is God and who is a devotee? This is not correct. The Semitics, Dravidians, and the Non-Aryans have thus deceived the whole human race for so long years. They are anti-Vedas. This prejudice has become a permanent factor among the human race. So to eradicate those prejudices, my form has been manifested within you eradicating all the past prejudices and that proof is borne by you.

Listen, The Munis, the Rishis, Godhood are all different stages of the human race in the spiritual world. These are all confined in individualism. But when a man is transformed into Brahma or Supreme Being becomes 'Paramatma' or 'Supreme Soul', then he remains as 'One' within the whole human race. None knows this natural and spontaneous phenomenon of the human race. Even they don't know about Spinoza's Nature, though he mentioned it in the macrocosm. But here it is in the microcosm.

This knowledge of oneness does not belong to individualism. The world gives the proof, when they say, 'We have seen you within me'. After this knowledge, he becomes a wise man. It means that I come to know that I am this human race – 'All is One and One is All' (Pantheism) You term it as a Human-religion. Can you think, that when the Rishis of this country are saying: 'Amritasya Putrah' (son of Immortal), 'Aham Brahmasmi' (I am Brahma), 'Tatvamasi' (Thou art that), what we are doing in the name of Religion! And see that Justice Woodroffe! being a foreigner, how did he conceive this human body in his book 'Serpent power! One thing you should know – the complete eradication of all prejudices is called the knowledge of Supreme Being (Brahmajnan). And this is 'Oneness' where there is no devotee, no God. There exists only 'He is one'.

[Brihad Aranyaka Upanishad mentions about such person as:

"He who has found and has awakened to the soul (self),
The world is his, indeed, he is the world itself". (4.4.13)

THE AUSTERITY OF THE EARTH – ITS MANIFESTATION IN JIBANKRISHNA'S BODY AND EFFECT

16.7/17.7. 1961

I was reading the book 'The Serpent Power' by John Woodroffe. He understood one thing. He is saying, whatever is on the outside is within this body. He has considered this human body. Today I shall tell you one thing from this book though he could not say properly.

Some days back I told you that I saw in my dream my own foot. As soon as I read that he has mentioned foot as earth, I conceived it. As soon as Dhiren came, I asked him the meaning of food, instantly he answered, 'You have seen the foot of Lord Vishnu'. What is written in the scriptures? Vishnu covered the world with his single leg. It means it shows that I have covered the whole world.

However, what is the meaning of this dream? Well, what have I told you? From where my spiritual life begins?' From this 'Pranamaya Kosha' (third plane), isn't so? What I saw in the fourth plane (Heart) - Aura. Then in the fifth plane, I saw air in the seventh plane I saw outer space, and then what remains there? Earth. I saw my foot – it means I saw the earth. And John Woodroffe has mentioned this foot as earth. What a wonderful thing it is! A long time back I saw water in Pranamaya Kosha and after a gap of so long years, I saw the earth.

The austerity of this earth was continuing within my body and due to its effect, I have this realization. Earth is the lowest zone of the planes and these are called the five elements which have come under my control. It is termed as 'Bhutasiddhi' in the scripture and it means 'control over the five elements.'

[Thousands of years ago Svetasvatara Upanishad has mentioned this austerity of the earth thus:

"When the five-fold quality of yoga has been produced,
Arising from the earth, water, fire, air, and space,
No sickness, no old age, no death has he, who has obtained a body made of the fire of yoga". (2.12)

'SVENA-RUPENA-ABHINISPADYATE' / 'PARAMJYOTI' AS PER UPANISHAD IS JUDICIOUS BUT IN THE LIFE OF JIBANKISHNA IT IS REALISTIC

18.7.1961

What the writers have said about the religious books is judicial. You say which Rishi has visualized 'Paramjyoti' (The

Supreme Light) and who has attained the state of 'Svena-Rupena Abhinispadyate' (transforming its own form into others) and where is the proof? But what has happened here? This book (Religion and Realization) is based on my personal revelations. This is the first and the last book in world history based on personal revelations because henceforth none will have the lower zone (Below sixth plane) realizations in the future. In reality, no Full-fledged individualistic visualization of God will happen. Thakur (Sri Ramakrishna) has given the criteria about visualizing God. But what is the specialty in the visualization of God in reality? During the time of visualizing God, no sense persists about the movement of Kundalini or Life-power. The seer sees only divine lights all around. And within that light, I am only seeing Thakur (Sri Ramkrishna) showing me the thumb-like lump of light with his finger (extending the hand) and saying – 'This is God! This is seeing God'! Thakur is within that divine light and so I am. What do you suppose? Was it physical Jibankrishna? No! I am then transformed into Pure Atma. Then Thakur merged into that divine light. And what was this God? I saw that inside that divine light there was another more powerful lump of light demarcated by a fine bluish light, almost in the shape of a thumb, and this is God.

Gita could not describe visualization of God and what they have said, they have taken it from Upanishad.

What did I see? I saw that a divine light emerging from 'Muladhara' (The root of the five sheaths) like a flash reached the sixth plane and then as soon as reached the cerebrum, it flashed up to the sixth plane. Though it is taking time to describe, the whole phenomenon happens in the twinkling of an eye.

Remember, Religion is based on Yoga. It is not inferential or imaginary. And Yoga means Rajyoga. That means the spontaneous revelation of self, not by self-exertion.

[This Atma or Soul is mentioned in Maitri Upanishad as such:

"Of size of thumb or span within the body,

A light of twofold or threefold brightness,

This Brahma who is being praised,

The Great God, - He has entered in all beings"! [6.38]

MAN IS BRAHMA OR SUPREME BEING – PAST, PRESENT, AND FUTURE ARE IN THE HUMAN BRAIN

On 20.7.1961, Diamond said:

This living human being is Brahma, not the dead one. When a man dies he becomes merged in infinity. This whole universe is within a human brain. The past, the present, and the future all are within this brain. One form of that is vast and another form is in seed form. How do you get its proof? Let me prove it – At my 12 years 4 months of age I saw in my dream Thakur (Sri Ramkrishna); then I saw Swamiji (Swami Vivekananda) in a dream. What happened? The past was shown to me within my brain. Didn't any of you see the past in a dream? Surely you have seen, and so the present and future also.

[Svetasvatara Upanishad has mentioned about the past, present, and future thus:

"The past, the future, and what the Vedas declare –

This whole world the illusion maker projects out of this (Brahma)". (4.9)

Again about the vast and seed form Svetasvatar Upanishad has mentioned

"More minute than the minute, greater than the great, Is the soul (Atman) that is set in the heart (cerebrum) of a creature here". (3.20)

THE 'PARAVIDYA' OR THE SUPREME CULT HAS

MANIFESTED IN JIBANKRISHNA WITH PROOF

24.7.1961

In Kaivalya pada of 'Patanjal Darshan' it is mentioned that Nature has no right on such Yogi and he becomes a liberated person.

Now I am showing you the difference. What is the difference? Between Semitic and Aryan Cult', because to some extent, it carries the sense of self-exertion. Better I should use the term 'Para Vidya' (or Supreme Cult). In his own case, Thakur (Sri Ramkrishna) is mentioning knowledge and devotion, and in the case of Sri Chaitanya distributed devotion to all casts. Now you see how Thakur has mentioned the difference between him and Sri Chaitanya!

Now, come to the main issue. 'There is no right of Nature on that yogi', which means he is then transformed into Purusha (Male). In his book 'Religion of mankind' Rabindra Nath Tagore has mentioned that the barrier of Nature could not hold him'. Though he said these intellectually from Upanishads. But what Patanjali has said? Who has become liberated after getting the state of 'Kaivalya'!

Now leaving aside from Thakur, I am mentioning the quote of the Rishi, 'I am Brahma' (Supreme Being). But as he said himself, so his words were not accepted by the world. What is the proof of that? Then he could not otherwise mention 'The question of Brahma or Supreme Being'.

But what I have told you so many times? Truth comes from the reverse. My life is such, otherwise – 'I am telling you, and you believe it'. There is no question of the term 'Faith' in religion. Its proof should be borne by the world without your knowledge, what you are seeing in your eyes here. Am I going to you for proof that I have become such? Or have I asked you, 'Have you seen me in a dream?" On the contrary, you have seen me and you are bearing the proof. And seeing me within you, you are transformed into Purusha (Person) irrespective of genders. You have not become the slave of that Purusha on the contrary you have become one with him.

[Katha Upanishad has mentioned that the inner Soul is inside and also outside with form in the hymn:

"As the one fire has entered the world
And becomes corresponding in form to every form
So the one Inner Soul of all things
Is corresponding in form to every form,
And yet is outside". (5.4)]

ANY OUTSIDE SIGNS OF A MAN IS AN OBSTACLE FROM ACHIEVING THE KNOWLEDGE OF ONENESS

28.7.1961

See I have introspection in my brain. I understood that Mahaprabhu (Sri Chaitanya of the fifteenth Century of Bengal who was a founder of Vaisnava Cult during Muslim reign) understood his fault of taking red-ochre cloth; Swamiji (Swami Vivekananda) also understood it. Why only special dresses, even in Upanishad they are against any outside signs for achieving the Supreme cult.

This cult is donated by the human race by seeing a living human being within themselves. So this won't to if I announce it about my achievement of oneness. The human race is seeing my form within them and announcing that they and I am one. And this is the only proof of oneness which we have achieved here, and which is the first time happened in the world. Even 'Pantheism' and 'Kashmiri Saivism' have not mentioned such a concrete example. Not only that, no annotator of Upanishads even has ever set an example of the hymns. But all of a sudden we have got such a miraculous thing.

[About outside signs, Mundaka Upanishad has mentioned:

"Soul or Atma cannot be obtainable) Not by sign is it grasped, not even by speech,

Not by any other sense-organs, austerity or work". (3.2.8)]

REVIVAL OF PRIMORDIAL RELIGION (VEDIC TRUTH) – JIBANKRISHNA'S REAL DIVINE LIFE

15.12.1961

Listen! The religion of the Rishis or the primordial religion of Upanishads is manifested here. Here the Life divine is established in a true to sense. If anyone achieves Divine life, then innumerable people will see him within themselves like this.

Oh! How wonderful is Rabindranath Tagore! He has considered living human beings during his explanations of Upanishads. For this reason, he used the term 'Human religion'. He has forecasted this phenomenon.

[Chandogya Upanishad says:

"And thus the Blessed man, rising from the lower physical Plane (to the seventh plane) attains the Supreme Light, and in his own form made of God's Light, appears within myriads of people to prove his attainment of the Supreme Light or the Brahmahood, as He is the Perfect and the Supreme One". (8.12.3)

THE QUESTION OF THE UPANISHAD ERA IS SOLVED IN JIBANKRISHNA'S ERA

21.12.1961

The Rishis with their great intellectualism said, 'Listen, the sons of immortals'. Then said, 'That art Thou' and in advance again said 'I am Brahma'. Well! Is that all? So this question is left – the whole human race in front of me – who are they? But what we are getting here? I and the whole human race in front of me are one, though many outside but 'one' inside. What is our heritage? Vedas? Upanishads? No! Our heritage is 'Rajyoga' (spontaneous evolution of self).

[Katha Upanishad says:

"The Inner Soul (Antaratma) of all things,
Who makes his one form manifold
Is performing a piece of supernatural magic
In appearing as many". (5.12)

JIBANKRISHNA – THE FUTURE RULER OF THE SPIRITUAL WORLD - THE CAUSE

20.1.1962

The book 'Kashmir Shaivism' has classified the esoteric condition of a human being – Param shiva, Shiva-Shakti, Sadashiv, Iswartatwa, and Sadashivtatwa or Sadakhyatatwa. Paramshiva – esoteric condition of a man; Shiva-Shakri this body-both physical body and the esoteric condition i.e., this physical body and Atma or soul; Sadashiva within this human body, there is always a hilarity flowing perpetual bliss and prosperity; Iswartatwa – I am this human race and Sadvidyatatwa – All these I am i.e., one is all and all is one. Here they have finished, and could not say the next stage. But I have understood that there are things above it and that is this controlling power of a human being within a man there is a possibility to achieve control over the world.

Just see, a few days back, at noontime I had a deep meditation and saw a man named 'Dakshina' – the most insignificant man seen last forty-two years ago. He used to live in the same lane though I had no introduction to him. I only knew that he was called Dakshina by the neighbors.

Just imagine forty-two years back I saw him last and I forgot him totally but he appeared in my meditation without my any intention to see him. As soon as I told others in my room, Dhiren told me that there was a reference to a meditation on 'Dakshina' by god Shankar or Mahadeb. He brought the book and I told Khitish to read it at his home. The next day I asked him, 'What have you understood'? He said, 'yes, this reference indicated this hymn as the ruler of the world'.

I also understood that this indicated the same meaning. When I was thinking about this meaning suddenly the form of Gopal (a companion) appeared before me – double action. I was thinking about my aspect but another one appeared before me. I could not keep quiet. So I asked them, 'can you say why I saw Gopal'? Khitish said, 'Go' (Cow) means the world, 'pal' means to nurture. It means who rules the world'.

I also thought about the hymns of Vedas – 'Rudra jatte Dakshinamukham tena pang pahi nityam'. 'Well, can we consider the term 'nurture' as to control'? Dhiren said, 'yes, it can be'. Well, now this Rudra (Destroyer) – who are they? Then we have to back to history. What do we get in history? We get these warlords like Alexander, Caesar, Ptolemy, Attila, Kaizer. What did Alexander want? He wanted to bring the humanities under his control of him. He realized that if he could bring all under the rule of a single man, then only there will be peace, prosperity, and happiness in the world. We also find in case of the Emperor Ashoka who wanted to bring all under his rule. But what we see in its place? Through these warlords, the world became full of sorrow instead of peace.

Now, why I was shown the form, 'Dakshina'? It means through this benevolence the actual peace will be showered on earth (Dakshina means who is benevolent).

[Brihad Aranyaka Upanishad has mentioned about such person attaining Godhood thus:

"He who has found and has awakened to the soul;

That has entered this conglomerate abode –

He is the maker of everything, for he is the creator of all;

The world is his; indeed, he is the world itself". (4.4.13)

Svetasvatar Upanishad is mentioning thus:

"When the five-fold quality of yoga has been produced; Arising from the earth, water, fire, air, and space; No sickness, no old age, no death has he; who has obtained a body out of the fire of yoga". (2.12)]

SEEING JIBANKRISHNA WITHIN THE BODY THE ETERNAL LACKING IS FULFILLED

On 8.4.1962 Diamond explained to the listeners: In the first chapter of Chandogya Upanishad they have mentioned about the Purusha (Supreme Person). They are explaining –

'Purusha' means who dwells in the cerebrum and accomplished the world with his own self. Now, let me ask you one question. Before coming here what was your lacking? To become one with me by seeing me within. I saw world tree within my cerebrum. That tree is sucking its food from my body. Again that tree exists within each human being. Seeing me within that, lacking will be fulfilled. And this is the concrete proof of that Purusha.

[Katha Upanishad mentions about the world tree rooted in Brahma as such:

Its root is above, its branches below – This eternal fig tree! That (root) is indeed is the Pure. That is Brahma. That indeed is called the Immortal. On it all the worlds do rest. And no one soever goes beyond it". (6.1)]

BRAHMA OR SUPREME BEING – THE DIVINE SELF OF THE HUMAN BEING – THE SELF OF BRAHMA IS BLISS

11.4.1962.

Brihad Aranyaka, Chandogya, Svetasvetara, Isha Upanishads have mentioned the phenomena happening here. They have mentioned many things about us. But actually, the writers did not have any experiences like ours. They have said that they have written on the basis of Sruti (on the basis of memories generation after generation). The actual phenomenon happened long, long years ago which cannot be conceived. But ultimately these did not last, and even it cannot be said whether this phenomenon will last or not. Brihad Aranyaka Upanishad has mentioned – Then 'He' can understand that He creates all. When this 'creates' and 'He' becomes merged, then He becomes the creator. When they are giving emphasis on the term 'He', it means they have considered a human being. Those who are knowledgeable can understand it. 'Knowledgeable' means knowledge of supreme cult and to understand all these, realizations are required, otherwise, nothing can be conceived.

How strange is my spiritual life! And this life has transformed the spiritual life of all into my spiritual life.

Now what is Brahma (Supreme Being)? He is your Divine Self. And the own self of Brahma is Bliss.

[Chandogya Upanishad says:

"The Soul (Atman) is the bridge (or dam), the separation for keeping these worlds apart. Over that bridge there cross neither day, nor night, nor old age, nor death, nor sorrow, nor well- doing, nor evil-doing.

All evils turn back therefrom, for that Brahma-world is freed from evil. Upon crossing that bridge, if one is blind, he becomes no longer blind; if he is sick, he becomes no longer sick, Upon crossing that bridge, the night appears even as the day, for that Brahma-world is ever illuminated". (8.4.1/2)

IN JIBANKRISHNA'S ERA THE SUPREME CULT WILL MANIFEST THROUGH THE BRAIN POWER UNLIKE THE PHYSICAL STRENGTH OF THE VEDIC ERA

21.5.1962.

This 'Paravidya' (Supreme Cult) has manifested now with the help of brainpower. In the Vedic era it used to manifest through physical strength as they used to say, 'Nayomatma Balahinena Lavyah' (Atma or soul cannot be seen by weaklings). But now it is different. Yesterday I said this, but I couldn't understand that I have already written it in the first part of my book 'Dharma-o-Anubhuti' (Bengali version). I understood a few moments back. I described that Babu (gentleman) is covered with cloth up to his neck (Diamond's dream). That dream indicated that the Supreme Cult will manifest through brainpower. I have seen this dream forty years back and that time I gave the meaning that nobody will have his austerity of the lower planes. After such a long period I got another meaning!

JIBANKRISHNA IS THE ADI PURUSH (THE GREAT PRIMEVAL MAN OF VEDAS)

3.6.1962

It is mentioned in Brihad Aranyaka Upanishad – In the beginning, He was alone in the shape of a person and this is the Adi Purush (the Great Primeval man) of Vedas. This means this phenomenon occurs encircling such man. Probably this phenomenon happened once thousands of years ago, and now we are seeing the same thing happening here. As you see my form within you, he is that most primeval man.

[Svetasvetara Upanishad has mentioned such a person like this:

"Without foot or hand, he is swift and a seizer! He sees without eye; he hears without ear! He knows whatever is to be known; him there is none who knows; Men call him the Great Primeval Person". (3.19)

[About this Primeval Person, two Muslim students saw dreams and are narrated below:

It was January 26, 1984. A local Muslim young man, student of 3rd year of Visvabharati, Santiniketan, Bolpur (Birbhum district of West Bengal, India) saw a series of dreams in five consecutive days.

On the first night, he saw that he was having a journey on an unknown road. On the second night, he saw one of his friends' hut on the last end of a high road. On the third night he saw Swami Vivekananda. On the fourth night, he saw that the wife of one of Jibankrishna's companions brought a dish of curd for him, and an unknown lady fed him the curd by spoon. On the fifth night, he saw a hilly road surrounded by forest. The surrounding was full of cow dung, stool, rotten mud and the primordial barbarian people were eating the decomposed meat of Pterodactyl, and took the extra meat with them. In the meantime, Jibankrishna came there and at once everything was clear. The people did not seem to be so barbarian.

Another Muslim young man saw in his dream that Jibankrishna is that Primeval man whose appearance started the manifestation of the civilization of mankind. They began to be civilized from the barbarian stage.]

MAN IS BRAHMA WITH PROOF –JIBANKRISHNA IS THE LIFE OF EVERY HUMAN BEING

5.6.1962

What is the sportive forms of life-power? I am enjoying the sportive forms of life-power with my form within you. What a wonderful phenomenon! How wonderful is this human body! How can I explain to you how wonderful this human body is! There is no language to explain it. We are the blessed ones who have come to this earth with this human body! Our life is fulfilled! We have realized what is the immense power of this human body! Don't take anything, only think why so many people are seeing a man within them!

You have seen me within you. Then what is happening? When you are seeing a person within you besides your existence, it proves that you are in existence. As you have seen one within you is borne by the proof of all these people present here. They are giving the same proof when you are casting your eyes outside. What does it mean? This bears the proof that man is Brahma (one). Listen, I have no eyes. I see through you! You are seeing me and after your narration, I can see. Both seeing and listening are identical as mentioned in Patanjali.

THE EXISTENCE OF THE PERSON OF BRAHMAPUR OR CEREBRUM IS PROVED

8.6.1962,

In the scriptures what is said? If anyone worships a symbol, he is confined within the symbol. And if one has his austerity without a symbol, then a person comes from Brahmapur (seventh plane or cerebrum). Then what does he do? He takes the seer to Brahmapur. You all know that the person comes from Brahmapur. From where does God-the-Preceptor come? From 'Nigam' (Descent).

So far nobody knows what is Brahmagyan (Supreme Cult). These European scholars have translated Vedas and Upanishads and what they have understood? When they have translated that person comes from Brahmapur, they thought that these are a myth. But what are you seeing here? We have seen that these are true, of course, who will understand all these? Unless anyone has realizations, he will not conceive all these.

[It has the reference in Katha Upanishad like this:

"He who is awake in those that sleep,
The Person who fashions desire after desire –
That indeed is the Pure. That is Brahma.

That indeed is called the Immortal.

On it all the worlds do rest;

And no one soever goes beyond it". (5.8)

How this hymn has manifested after thousands of years will be revealed by this dream seen by

Ms Smriti Banerjee who is a listener of Chetla Reading Centre and narrated her dream.

"In my dream, I saw that JIbankrishna was showing his thumb and addressing me said, 'She has visualized God.' I said, 'But He comes from Brahmapur' (cerebrum). He said, 'I have come from that Brahmapur.' The dream was off."]

DISCARDING ALL THE STATES OF AUSTERITY BY JIBANKRISHNA

11.6.1962.

I am the most ordinary man, but still, people are seeing me in the sun. Firstly, Abhay saw me in sun in his dream and when he narrated to me, I thought, what an imagination! But after a long time when I got Isha Upanishad in my hand, I saw that they have mentioned the man in the sun.

At present, my state is the state of a primeval man of the Vedas. But still, I could not stick to any state for so long.

Why I could not accept? It is because if anyone has lacking he will accept, otherwise not.

THE SYMPTOM OF 'BHUMA' (UNIVERSAL) AND THE ULTIMATE RESULT OF ACHIEVING 'BHUMANANDA' (UNIVERSAL BLISS)

15.6.1962.

So long Upanishad has only mentioned 'Bhuma', but could not say what is it. And seeing (in my dream) that papaya and a man Bhumanada I have understood what is it. I have now understood what is 'Bhumaiba sukham' (Perpetual happiness).

The papaya has many seeds. This means that I see you all now within me. This is called Bhuma. It has been mentioned in Kashmiri Shavaism as 'Sadakhyatatwa'. And what is 'Sadvidyatatwa'? – One is all, all is one......But Kashmiri Shaivism could not say all these things that have happened here. This has manifested within my body, though without my knowledge and I don't know A, B, C of these. I can give you a rational explanation that for the last five thousand years what has not manifested in anybody's brain is manifested within my brain. My brain has created that papaya and then makes me understand that this is

'Bhumananda' (Supreme Joy). What a strange thing that nobody has achieved this for the last five thousand years! You have seen me i.e., mango with a single seed – you have 'Brahmananda' (Individualistic) and I see you all within me – the papaya with many seeds – I have 'Bhumananda' (Universal joy or bliss of Brahma)

[Taittiriya Upanishad has mentioned thus:

"Wherefrom words turn back; Together with the mind; not having attained; the bliss of Brahma he who knows; Fears not from anything at all". (2.9)]

UPANISHAD HAS BECOME PERSONIFIED IN JIBANKRISHNA'S ERA

27.7.1962

'Tatva-jnana' ('You are Thy') means 'Atma-jnana' (I am Thy) and this proof will be borne by the world. He himself will not know it. That will be mentioned by the human race. This universalism is proof of Godhood. This is mentioned by Upanishad. What we have achieved here is mentioned in Upanishads. What they have said has manifested here and I am not saying so, you are saying. And this Upanishad has mentioned your stage of perpetual peace. Those who have seen me within, have achieved perpetual peace and happiness. And what happens after this achievement? This is getting me inside. Outside there are many but inside 'one' exists only. And to see 'one' inside is the knowledge which is never lost. You will remember it forever. Would you disbelieve that you have seen me within you? No! So it is eternal.

The religion of imagination creates incarnation and 'Paramhansa' and the religion of Upanishad creates 'Truth', which means perpetual peace and happiness. You are mentioned as 'Dhira' in Upanishads. Just think about what has happened here!

Having this the most precious thing here, our lives are fulfilled to the fullest extent. Here the religion of Upanishads is manifested. Mind that Religion is the perpetual motion of life-power within a human body.

JIBANKRISHNA – AN UNFATHOMABLE PERSON

2.1.1963

"I would have given you pen and paper saying, what have you understood about me'. But do you know I don't say that? Because I know there is none in this world who can explain this phenomenon. I cannot say whether anybody in future can explain it".

CAUSES OF EXPRESSION OF SUPREME CULT WITHIN JIBANKRISHNA

One day in the month of January 1963 Diamond said, "Why this cult has been expressed in my body? Can you explain it? Because 'Sa Uttama Purusha' – The best man. The best man in the midst of the human race. Have you understood? Now the question is whether this has been revealed after my birth or the beginning of my birth? Both are true."

This phenomenon has been mentioned in Aitareya Upanishad(5.4) like this about Rishi Bamdeva – 'So he, having ascended aloft from his world with that intelligent Self(Atman), obtained all desires in you heavenly world and became immortal – yea became immortal.'

THE FUNDAMENTAL THOUGHT OF VEDANTA IS ONENESS WHICH HAS MANIFESTED IN JIBANKRISHNA'S ERA

21.7.1964.

I have doubt whether anybody in the world has known, Atma or Supreme Soul. Upanishads are saying, 'Being transformed into Great Consciousness the seer transforms every human being into his own form'.

In Vivekananda centenary Memorial volume; page 276, Swami Vivekananda has mentioned – The central idea of Vedanta is oneness. There are no two in anything – no two lives, there is only one life, one world, one existence, everything is that one. The difference is in degree and not in kind".

So the fundamental idea of Vedanta is oneness. Listen, what was only the concept or idea to them, that is a fact and truth to us.

JIBANKRISHNA IS THE 'UTTAMA PURUSHA' OR THE BEST MAN AS MENTIONED IN UPANISHAD

24.7.1964

What do you do with oracles? You hear it. This may be called 'Sruti' (means to keep in memory after a hearing). The other name of Vedas is Sruti (because hearing through generation after generation the Rishis or sages codified the Vedas). Now the question is who heard it? He is that Uttam Purusha or the Best Man. Then that Purusha was manifested as an oracle and at the same time, he was the listener! If you say, how! The listener was the Rishi who heard this oracle. Why had he returned to Atma or Soul? he said, 'He is that best man and he is the Soul' And prior to that, he said, 'And thus This Man, rising from the lower plane to the seventh plane, attains the supreme light, and by His own form made of God's light, appears within myriads of people to prove His attainment of 'Brahmatva or the Brahmahood, as He is the perfect and the 'Supreme One'. Why did not one and all scholars, all intellectuals, all religious teachers mention the Soul within the human body? Why did none of them prove that He himself is the Soul including this body? Both Soul and person are identical. So, why did none of them become that 'Purusha' or person who could be the form of every human being? This proves that the inner person is the listener. For so many centuries that unknown person was the listener. Now that person achieved the body of flesh and blood. The form of a living human being has become the speaker within a human body and listener outside while the speaker is the human race. Because unless you tell me, I don't know anything. I knew myself through you. For this reason, I always say, 'You are my masters, my God'. And you see, so long that 'Person' remained in embryo stage within those Rishis and great Religious Teachers and in embryo stage there cannot be any austerities in full-fledged from. For this purpose, a suitable human body is required. And this is that body. Now you say whether Vedas have mentioned the past or the future? That proof is already in Vedas – 'A man in the sun'. Who is that man? So many people of all ages and gendrs have seen me in the sun in their dreams. What is that sun? This life. So long the sun will be there, the human race will see me within them and I shall live with this form. There is no destruction of 'Brahmavidya' (knowledge of Supreme One). Vedas have mentioned 'Those who have known and seen Him, get perpetual peace and happiness.' I had no idea about this but have witnessed it lifelong. It was already in existence, only discovered. A living human being could not become 'Brahma' (one) in the past, but the 'Truth' is discovered through me. And you are proving that, saying, 'you are that Brahma or one'.

[We find in Isha Upanishad where the Vedic sage is praying: "O Nourisher (Pusan), the sole Seer (Ekarsi), O Controller (Yama), O Sun (Surya), offspring of Prajapati, spread forth thy rays! Gather thy brilliance (Tejas),! What is thy fairest form – that of thee I see. He who is yonder, yonder Person (Purusha) – I myself am he"! [16]

BRAHMA OR SUPREME BEING IS BEYOND THE THREE ATTRIBUTES – SATVA, RAJAH, TAMAH (GOODNESS-ACTIVENESS-DARKNESS)

One day in the month of December 1964, Diamond said: Brahma is beyond the three attributes. These are Satva, Rajah, and Tamah. I have achieved this Brahmahood and what I am seeing? Thieves, anti-socials, drunkards, honest, and dishonest men, ruffians, barbers, washer-men, scholars, and many others are achieving this Brahmahood through me.

A ruffian of Posta had come to me along with his companions. Sitting here they had discussions with me. Then at the time of departure, they said, 'Last night I saw you in the dream with all the houses, trees, etc.' Then I understood that this is proof that Brahma is beyond the three attributes.

[In this context Svetasvatar Upanishad has mentioned as such:

"The one God, hidden in all things,

All-pervading, the Inner soul of all things, the overseer of deeds in all things abiding, the witness, the sole thinker, devoid of qualities".]

VISUALIZATION OF GOD BY JIBANKRISHNA

One day in December 1964 Diamond said -

The most wonderful contribution of Sri Ramkrishna to the world when he said very specifically, 'I swear that I have seen God' – nobody has ever said these words to the world. In Brihadaranyaka Upanishad Jajnabalka mentioned this as 'Atma or soul can be seen and heard etc.' He was using the word 'can' or 'should'. It means whether he had seen God or not. Then, coming to Svetasvatar Upanishad, we find these words, "I know this mighty Person (Purusha) of the color of the Sun, beyond the darkness. Only by knowing Him does one pass over death. There is no other path for going there". (3.8)

I had this vision and I knew it. And I have pointed it out in the third part of my book 'Religion and Realization'. I have mentioned that this is not the actual visualization of God or Brahma. This is a visualization of Yogic form when the life power or Kundalini comes suddenly to the mid eyebrow and from there goes to the cerebrum straight. Then a flash of this Divine Consciousness is seen from the cerebrum to the throat. I have mentioned under it that this is not the actual visualization of God. God is seen in trinity and I have explained it as many may think that this is the proper visualization of God. As, Sri Ramkrishna is mentioning in the 'Gospel of Sri Ramkrishna' that some unknown person will come, just as he came in my case, and at that time he was unknown to me. Though, when he was showing me God in my cerebrum, he was not unknown to me. For this reason, I have mentioned in my book that God-the-Preceptor or the Holy Ghost comes and shows God. Therefore I have seen him many times and he was shown me so many things. What does it mean? This is, 'when He wishes He is seen'. It is my own divine consciousness – imperceptibly made its way to the cerebrum and there assumed the form of Thakur (Sri Ramkrishna) and came down to me again and carried me there in Brahmapur (cerebrum) – In brief, I have described it.

TAITTIRIYA UPANISHAD DESCRIBES 'BRAHMA' IN THE MACROCOSM - IT IS IN THE MICROCOSM IN JIBANKRISHNA

December 1964

Taittiriya Upanishad is saying 'He deserves that I shall become many and take birth'. But come to me! In my lifetime you innumerable in number are giving birth to my form within you – do I deserve this! How can I? I had no idea about it, how the question of 'deserving' will come? Then you have seen me, narrated to me, so I have understood that I have become many. The same phenomenon reverberated in Swami Vivekananda's quote 'I have become many to see my own form'. So why such anomalies in Taittiriya Upanishad that He will become many? Because they are keeping Brahma outside – in the macrocosm. And we are saying the same thing in microcosm i.e., in the esoteric condition, within our bodies what is happening in reality.

[Taittiriya Upanishad says –

"He desired: Would that I was many! Let me procreate myself".]

THE PERSON IN BRAHMAPUR IS THE SOUL OR ATMA – IN THE FORM OF JIBANKRISHNA

Diamond said one day:

There is another person within this human body and He is Brahma (or Supreme Being). Vedas have mentioned that there is a person in Brahmapur (cerebrum) and He should be visualized. Within the causal body that Person appears in the form of goddess Kali, Krishna, sometimes as Jesus Christ, Muhammed, Sri Ramkrishna, or Sri Chaitanya and tries to teach the seer that 'I am all these. Because there is no 'Two', there is only 'one'.

[Katha Upanishad has mentioned about this person thus:

"He who is awake in those that sleep,
The Person who fashions desire after desire -
That indeed is the Pure. That is Brahma.
That indeed is called the Immortal.
On it all the worlds do rest;
And no one soever goes beyond it". (5.8)

JIBANKRISHNA'S FORM IS IN EXISTENCE IN EVERY HUMAN BEING AS PARAMATMA OR SUPREME BEING

Diamond said one day:

Thakur (Sri Ramkrishna) used to say, 'To donate food and education comes under the inferior category. To donate knowledge is superior to the two. I have donated myself to you. Whatever I have achieved I have donated that to you. As you see me within you and have realizations, I cannot know anything about that, unless you come and inform me. This means that you have been transformed into me (in the spiritual world). Why I have donated all of my attributes? Is it for my interest? No, from within you I shall enjoy myself. I don't take anything and always go for negation – this is an idealism', the effect of which we are seeing here.

As 'Bibhu' my form is manifested in so many people. Bibhu means 'Paramatma' or 'Supreme Being'.

[In this context Svetasvetara Upanishad has mentioned like this:

"The one God, hidden in all things,
All-pervading, the Inner Soul of all things,
The overseer of deeds, in all things, abiding,
The witness, the sole thinker, is devoid of qualities". (6.11)

JIBANKRISHNA WITH THOUSAND HEADS, EYES AS MENTIONED IN UPANISHADS – ITS REAL MEANING

[Svetasvatara Upanishad has mentioned about the Person with thousand heads and thousand eyes thus:

The Person has a thousand heads;
A thousand eyes, a thousand feet;
He surrounds the earth on all sides,
And stands ten fingers' breadth beyond. (3.14)

Again Svetasvetara Upanishad says:

'Who is the face, the head, the neck of all,
Who dwells in the heart of all things,
All-pervading is He, and bountiful;

Therefore omnipotent and kindly (Siva)". (3.11)

On 12.5.1962 Diamond discussed:

See, Chitta has a dream. He was seeing that I was affected by smallpox and even flies were sitting on my body. He asked me, 'Are you suffering from smallpox'? I didn't answer him. But later on, he said, 'No, that was not smallpox. Those were eyes as seen on pineapple'.

Hearing this Dhiren Roy said, 'In Purus Sukta of Rig Veda' they have described a person with thousands of heads, thousands of eyes, thousands of hands'. Chitta's dream has indicated that you are that Purusha (Person). Again Aitareya Upanishad has mentioned, that Purusha has disappeared. It means that the Purusha who appeared once were never seen later on. And his memory has been carried by 'Sruti' (Later Upanishads). From that era, this expectation has been borne by people of all countries. So Buddha is called 'Tathagata' (He will come)' Christ is called 'one is to come', Mohammed is saying, 'I am the prophet of Allah', Sri Chaitanya is saying, 'I am he', and Thakur (Sri Ramkrishna) is saying, 'He who is Ram is Krishna and now is Ramkrishna'.

Diamond exclaimed, well said! well said! you have explained the thing so wonderfully! But my boy, as you said, 'That

Purusha appeared once and later on he was not seen. Now, where did he appear? Of course not in the outer world, otherwise his name was found with his activities just as is found with other Rishis.

So, it is merely a memory. It means, this memory appeared in some Rishis and whatever yogic stages it might be, yet that phenomenon appeared only in memory and so in due course of time it disappeared. Now if you say that the ever-desired person has appeared now with flesh and blood, it will not disappear ever. This will continue perpetually, even after physical death. Because that Purusha is not merely a memory but a living human being.

After a few days of this discussion on 16th May 1962, Wednesday discussions were going on about a dream seen by Dwijendra Nath Roy of Ghatshila (Bihar, India).

Diamond said, see, "he didn't know anything about the discussions going on here. He has written a letter to his next brother Sailen".

The letter was written on 14.5.1962 and Mr. Roy saw the dream on 7.5.1962. The dream was such:

From a single throat, innumerable faces were revolving like a disc. The middle face belonged to Jibankrishna and over it, the head of Sri Ramkrishna was seen. Both of their heads were fixed but all the heads known and unknown were revolving. It was just like the picture of Ravana with ten heads, though the number of heads was countless, and this scene did not seem to be unusual. Numerous heads were seen and then vanishing with the appearance of more new faces irrespective of old, child, and young, known and unknown and all the faces were continuously revolving except the faces of Jibankrishna and Ramkrishna which were smiling and luminous. Among these faces, my face was also there. The dream may indicate universal oneness. If you find any other meaning, write to me.

Hearing this dream Dhiren said, 'That day we discussed this matter on thousand heads. But the strange thing is that my brother was in Ghatshila and he had no idea that we were discussing this phenomenon. Still, he had seen such a dream!

Diamond asked Dhiren, 'Well Vedas mentioned any symptoms of that lost person?'

Dhiren said - yes, about the symptoms, they are saying, 'That Purusha has thousands of heads, thousands of eyes'.

Diamond – Well, now can you prove that I have a thousand eyes?

Dhiren – Yes, so many people are seeing you within their dreams. Where are they? All are you and their eyes are yours.

Diamond – Yes, my boy! This is with proof.

[Brihad Aranyaka upanishad has mentioned:

"This mankind is honey for all things and all things are honey for this mankind. This shining immortal Person who is in this mankind, and, with reference to oneself, this shining immortal person who exists as a human being - he is just this Soul, this Immortal, this Brahma, this All".]

COMMITMENTS OF JIBANKRISHNA TO COMPLETE INCOMPLETE VEDAS

19.5.1965

It is written in Hindu religious books that out of four parts of Brahma only one part is exposed. The rest three parts are yet in dark. That one part is Veda. But that one part was not said completely. Though instead of four parts there are five parts, out of which Veda is an incomplete part. The rest four parts I shall expose and write.

'BRAHMA' AS MENTIONED IN VEDAS IS A LIVING HUMAN BEING – MAN IS THE ETERNAL TRUTH

One day Diamond said - You know, that I saw in my vision that I will illuminate the whole world with 'Oneness', and now you have proved it. I have never crossed anybody's door. On the contrary, you have come to me and said, 'we have seen you within us'. This is not done by me. You have seen and you have done all these. I am not concerned at all. Everything happening here is automatic. People of all religions are seeing me within themselves. It means all religions are becoming one, and there is no difference.

In every religion there is incarnation. Gabriel said to Mohammed, 'you are the Prophet', Jesus said, 'I am the son of God'; Buddha was termed as 'one is to come'. But Sri Ramkrishna said, 'Incarnation is a proven one. There is mankind within the body of a man', and also said, 'I am seeing everyone as Ram. But no one saw him. Only he saw and people may not believe it. But here all of you are seeing that you are one (in one point). Ram means 'one' i.e., Brahma and the man you are seeing within you is a living human being. Then 'Brahma' is a living human being! When you are seeing me within you, you are transforming into me. Thus all of you are becoming one.

Sri Ramkrishna mentioned man as the best creature on earth. But before him, Chandidas (a saint and a creator of many devotional lyrics in Bengal in mid centuries) has mentioned like this: 'The Truth above all is Man and nothing is there above that'. My boys, this man is Brahma or the Truth. And here is the full definition of Brahma. If everybody is one, then there is no necessity of incarnation or devotees. And here it exceeds all the past religions.

[Katha Upanishad has described the Person or Purusha as the highest course thus:

"Higher than the senses are the objects of sense,
Higher than the objects of senses is the mind;
And higher than the mind is the intellect.
Higher than the intellect is the Great Self (Atman).
Higher than the Great is the Unmanifest (avyakta),
Higher than the Unmanifest is the Person.
Higher than the Person there is nothing at all.
That is the goal. That is the highest course". (3.10-11)]

PART 2 JIBANKRISHNA THE MAN IN THE SUN MENTIONED BY UPANISHAD

Man in the sun – Who is He

Jibankrishna explained thus:

A man becomes God, but spiritually or otherwise physically he is but a man like you. He is seen within by thousands. The man seen within by thousands becomes Absolute and the seers see the Leela (sportive forms of God) within the body.

According to the Isha Upanishad, the man seen is the 'Man in the sun' and seers see Him in their own 'Gold-sheath' (Hiranmoy Kosha as mentioned in Upanishad). The sun is the symbol of life power in the seventh plane and some 30 men and women have seen 'Diamond' within them.

It may be taken as Plato's 'Absolute Equality' and Abstract Equality'.

Five of the Upanishads: 1) Brihad Aranyaka, 2) Chandogya, 3) Maitri, 4) Taittiriya, and 5) Isha point out the 'Man in the sun'. It is but a macrocosm; whereas, the thing actually takes place in the microcosm. The plain meaning is not in the outside world but in the human body. 'The sun' and the 'Man-in-the-sun' are seen. It is so experienced here by many but within their own cerebrum and reported to Jibankrishna. And they are some 30 or more. Even now it is running (1962-63).

CHAPTER 1 GOLDEN PERSON JIBANKRISHNA'S FORM IN THE SUN

The sun is the lifeline of this universe and within that sun the Supreme person or 'Parama Brahma' is seen. Who is He and what is He?

Chandogya Upanishad has mentioned Him as such:

"That Golden Person who is seen within the sun, has a golden beard and golden hair. He is exceedingly brilliant, all, even to the fingernail tips". [1.6.6]

One person has seen Jibankrishna in the sun in a dream and when he narrated it to Jibankrishna he quoted the above hymns to the dreamer and said," Have you heard that the person in sun is Brahma and you have seen Him, that means you are also transformed into Brahma. To see is to become."

Now Rishi (Sage) Jagyabalka said," Aham Brahmasmi" (I am Brahma). It means every human being is Brahma. Now the question comes how a person achieves Brahmahood? Jibankrishna said," The life force or Kundalini of a human body, through the process of Rajyoga is transformed into Brahma. To see is to become."

Now Rishi (sage) Jagyabalka said," Aham Brahmasmi" (I am Brahma). It means every human being is Brahma. Now the question comes how a person achieves Brahmahood? Jibankrishna said," The life force or Kundalini of a human body, through the process of Rajyoga is transformed into Brahma in the seventh plane after crossing five sheaths or seven planes. In whose body it occurs he also achieves Brahmahood, and the proof is borne by myriads of people after seeing him within their bodies. In individualism, the proof is faith, whereas in universalism it is reality.

Svetasvatara Upanishad says that this human being is the son of immortal as we find this hymn as such:

"I join your ancient prayer which adorations!
My verses go forth like suns upon their course,
All the sons of the Immortal listen,
Even those who ascended to heavenly stations!" (2.5)

THE FORM OF JIBANKRISHNA IN THE SUN AND IN THE PHYSICAL BODY IS THE SAME

On 28.12.1960 Diamond said:

Isha Upanishad is mentioning, 'Oh the Purusha (person) in the sun, check your rays let me see you. I am not praying to you, this is my birthright'. But Chandyogya Upanishad criticizing Isha is saying, 'That person is in your eyes not in the outside sun'. And the writer of the scripture made comments, 'Wherever the eyes cast, Lord Krishna is seen'. Even Thakur (Sri Ramkrishna) whenever he casts his eyes. But he could not understand that this consciousness was his causal body and he was seeing in his trance, otherwise he would have mentioned it.

But now what you have established? That Purusha is in the sun and that form is mine. Both the persons in the sun and Hiranmay Kosha are the same. It is not the outside sun and no person lives there. This sun means – the power of this human body – Life. The form of the life power of the whole human race is my form.

[Taittiriya Upanishad has mentioned thus:

Both he who is here in a person and he who is yonder in the sun – he is one. (2.8)]

THE FORM OF JIBANKRISHNA IN THE SUN IS ETERNAL

Diamond discussed one day in June 1958.

What a wonderful dream you saw Saila (Chakravarty)! Have you heard what has been written in Isa Upanishad? They said, 'The man in the Sun is Brahma' (Supreme One). And you have seen him! This means that you are also transformed into him. It was even written thousands of years before in Isa Upanishad. Then these realizations have been continuing through Sruti (By memorizing). Again after thousands of years, Upanishad was written and we are discussing this. But what they saw in sun could not say clearly. Here, as you are seeing my form in the sun, they could not say so specifically.

I knew that they saw this form. I knew that my form exists in the sun because that form is unchangeable. Though in Vedas what has been written was in the macrocosm. Everybody thought that the form would be seen in the outside sun in the sky. For these reasons Hindus Practice 'Tratak' (worshiping outside the sun by constantly looking at the sun). But with this practice, their eyes became fixed gaze or lost their eye-sight. Sri Ramkrishna also practiced it for six months and he got fixed gazed eyes. See the difference! Saila has said that he has seen my form in the sun within the body and Isa Upanishad has mentioned the outside sun.

See, I never used to read these types of books. But why I have brought these books now? Proof may be of three categories: - (1) Guessing; (2) Ascent and (3) Direct. The ascent proof is what Rishis (Sages) or Great Religious Teachers have said is to be accepted and the direct proof is the own realization. Your proofs are direct. Because you have seen yourselves in dreams my form. Now I am hearing that altogether 12-13 people have seen my form in the sun. These books are brought here to establish your direct proof with the ascent proof of the Vedic Rishis.

When you have seen my form in the sun, you have gained Supreme knowledge. Thereafter you have austerities of the lower planes. This is just opposite to Vedas or Tantras when they say that flowers first and then fruits. Why flowers? To produce fruits of Supreme knowledge. Here you have got first the Supreme knowledge whenever you have seen my form within yourselves.

MAN IN THE SUN IS VISUALIZED WITHIN THE BODY

24th June 1958.

Till now four persons have seen me in the sun within themselves. They are Saila, Kali, Santosh, and Abhay. Most of them told me about their dreams how many will I consider. Let these go on.

Now this man in the sun within the body is described in Isha Upanishad as 'Param Brahma'(Supreme One) They are describing – O Nourisher (Pusan), the sole Seer (Ekarsi), O controller (Yama), O Sun (Surya), offspring of Prajapati, spread forth thy rays! Gather thy brilliance (Tejas)! What is thy fairest form – that of thee I see. He who is yonder, yonder person (Purusha) – I myself am he! [16]

For a few days, I have been reading it. These four persons have seen that 'Param Brahma.' Isa Upanishad has 18 hymns. Only two of them have mentioned 'Param Brahma'. Just imagine how much importance they have given to it!

But two things they could not say. One, where this man in sun seen – whether outside or inside. And two, if they saw this person, who was this person and did he look?

See, Isha Upanishad also is making a mistake! They are saying that this person can be seen in the sun outside, and as a result what happens? Thousands and thousands of people tried to perform 'Tratak' to see that man on the outside (in India) and lost their eyesight. We can see this reference even in the life of Thakur (Sri Ramkrishna). He had also lost his eyesight by this process. Though by his spiritual power he got back his eyesight. Just imagine what harm did this Upanishad to mankind!

What Isha Upanishad could not say, these four persons have said. Each of them told me, 'We have seen a person in the sun in our dreams. And that person was you.'

Why could not Isha Upanishad say this clearly? Because what they have written was not visualized by them. Hearing from other persons they have written. They have also confessed that after hearing from others they have written it. For this reason, Upanishads are called 'Sruti'. They were merely scholars; not Rishis and they had no realizations like Rishis.

All IS ONE AND ONE IS ALL

27.7.1961

See, fourteen people including male and female have seen me so long in the sun in their dreams. What does it mean? The life power of human beings is me. I have accumulated the life force of the human race within me. And this I have recorded in my book 'Religion and Realization' a long time back. Long years have passed when I was shown in my dreams that the wheel-shaped circle with a rod was held in my hand. This wheel-shaped missile symbolizes kundalini or life-power.

The proof that I am the life-power of human being was bourne by you and still continues. So what has happened here? – All is one and one is All.

[In Chandyogya Upanishad it is mentioned about the person in sun as such:

'Now, that golden Person who is seen within the sun has a golden beard and golden hair. He is exceedingly brilliant, all, even to the fingernail tips. (1.6.6)]

Again they say:

'Earth, fire, food, sun are forms of me. But the Person, who is seen in the sun – I am he; I am He indeed'. (4.11.1)

THE MAN IN THE SUN IS INSIDE THE BODY

22.6.1962.

Well, these Rishis have mentioned in Upanishads about the man in the Sun – could they say where is this Sun? No! But here 14-15 people have seen the man in the sun – where have they seen? Within their bodies, not outside. You have seen me in dreams, isn't it? Then what does it matter? Rishis have said – 'He who dwells in the man, and he who dwells in the sun are one and the same,' why haven't they said that the sun is within this human body and the person dwells in that sun? It is because they have taken this sun outside and in place of that what you are saying? Yes, that man in the sun exists, but that is not outside, that is inside. Do you know what has happened? I am Truth and the Truth has revealed in me. The world is within me, and the Truth, what has been revealed in me has been revealed in the outside world simultaneously. And so what have you done? You have corrected the wrong interpretations of the Rishis and established the Truth. While Rishis have said that the sun and the man in the sun are outside, you have established that they are within the body. Then compare yourselves with those Rishis. You are the real Rishis. 'Rishis' means who visualize the Truth so what we have got here? Our human birth is fulfilled. We are born as human beings. On, we are honored by being human beings!

[Chandogya Upanishad has mentioned about the man in the sun thus:
Earth, fir, food, sun (are forms of me, But) the person who is seen in the sun – I am he, I am he indeed. (4.11.1)]

THE FORM OF JIBANKRISHNA IN THE SUN IS ETERNAL AND PERPETUAL

On 25.8.1962, Diamond said:

Here, so many people have seen me in the sun. King Bharat (as mentioned in Upanishads) was worshiping that man in the sun. Again Vedic Rishis was willing to see that man in the sun. So what does it mean? I am that man. King Bharat worshiped me. So I am eternal. I was in the past, I am in the present and will exist in the future. If the sun in the eras of king Bharat, Rishis, and the present is the same, then I am also the same. And so here three generations have seen me within themselves. Now if the fourth-generation sees me within, I shall accept it as correct.

[Taittiriya Upanishad has mentioned:

Both he who is here in a person and he who is yonder in the sun – he is one (2.8)]

THE CONSEQUENCE OF SEEING JIBANKRISHNA IN THE SUN

One day in the month of January 1963, Diamond said:

These people see me in the sun in dreams. What is it? Why they didn't see any other people in the sun? Had anybody seen Thakur (Sri Ramkrishna) in the sun? No, not at all! I have given you so many explanations for seeing me in the sun. Today listen to another explanation. As the whole world sees the sun, they will see my form one day. Showing me in the sun indicates that one day everybody throughout the world will see my form in the sun within their bodies.

CHAPTER 2 SEEING JIBANKRISHNA IN THE SUN IN HIS LIFETIME

[Quite a number of people have seen Jibankrishna or Diamond in the sun in dreams and trances both in his lifetime and after death. Even after his death in 1967, still, people see him in the sun through dreams and in trance. Such phenomenon has been mentioned in different Upanishads, though the person in the sun described by them remained unidentified. They have only mentioned in their hymns.

Then thousands and thousands of years rolled by, but that phenomenon remains a mystery to mankind and thousands of people in India have lost their eyes by looking at the outside sun to trace that person, But in vain!

After so long years Jibankrishna unveiled the mystery when the first man saw him in the sun in his dream. Thereafter as days passed by, countless people saw him in the sun through their dreams, and still, it is continuing. A very few examples are recorded to establish the truth described in Upanishads and discussed in the light of Jibankrishna's dialogues on different dates with reference to the hymns of Upanishads.]

FIRST MAN WHO SAW JIBANKRISHNA IN THE SUN IN DREAMS IN HIS LIFETIME

Abhaypada Mukherjee of Srirampur town, Hoogly district (West Bengal, India) first met Jibankrishna sometime in the year 1951.

On the third day of his meeting with Jibankrishna, he saw him in a dream as narrated by him.

I saw in my dream that the sun rises on the eastern side of a pond and Jibankrishna was seen inside the sun. On the other side of the pond, a sage seen a few days ago lying on a brittle cot was drowning inside the pond. Here the dream was off.

Isha Upanishad has mentioned about the man in the sun thus:

He who is yonder, yonder person in the sun – I myself is he. Verily that which is the sun hood of the sun is the Eternal Real. That is the pure, the personal, the sexless.
Of the bright power that pervades the sky, it is only a portion which is as it were, in the midst of the sun, in the eye, and in the fire. That is Brahma. That is the Immortal. That is splendor. That is the Eternal Real. (6.35)

November 23, 1954, Saturday.
Santosh Guchait narrated to Diamond about his dream today – 'Last night I dreamed that I was coming towards Dasnagar (Howrah) through the Rail line. It was then 7 am. Looking at the sun I saw that you are seated inside the sun, wearing a dhoti with a bare upper body, just like your present form.
Jibankrishna asked others about the meaning. One of them said – In Upanishad, this person is called the 'Parama Brahma' (Supreme self).

March 24, 1955, Sunday.
Upen Mukherjee narrated to Diamond (Jibankrishna) his wife's dream as such.

My wife is dreaming that you are sitting in the sun in the posture of Padmasan (a posture for meditation). Your head is clean shaved having a short beard and mustache.

Diamond – Oh, she has seen me in the sun! Pay my regard to her. She has blessed me after seeing me in the sun.

14, 1962.

A person named Tulsi from Baruipur (24-Parganas South of West Bengal State) told Diamond (Jibankrishna) – In meditation, I saw the sun and it was you. In front, a mirror was seen and so many forms of yours were reflected on it. You were then saying – 'Those, forms which you are seeing are the reflections of the sun'.

Diamond – what a strange matter! This is the Parama Brahma (Supreme Self) within the sun as mentioned in Upanishads.

CHAPTER 3 SEEING JIBANKRISHNA IN THE SUN IN DREAMS AFTER HIS DEATH

Debranjan Chatterjee is about nine years old and goes to listen to the reading of Diamond's Bengali book 'Dharma-O-Anubhuti' (Religion and Realization) at Sriniketan (Birbhum, West Bengal, India) reading Center.

After 2-3 days of listening to the reading, he began to dream about Jibankrisna in various ways.

He narrated one of his dreams as such:

05.08.1992, I saw that a swan was swimming in a pond. Suddenly it was transformed into Jibankrishna. I was very surprised to see this scene. I asked him, 'who are you?' He said, 'I am the sun.' I asked, 'Then where are your rays'? He said, 'will you see.' As soon as I said, 'Yes', he was transformed into a sun. Inside it a lotus was seen and on it Jibankrishna was having a meditation. From his body, dazzling light was emerging. He said, 'see it'! And my dream was off.

[Lotus – Seventh plane or cerebrum; Sun – Life i.e., Jibankrishna (Life+Krishna). He is seen in the Sun.

Upanishad has mentioned that the person in the Sun is Parama-Brahma or the Supreme Being.]

Partha Ghosh of Tala Park, Kolkata first came to know the name of Jibankrishna at Balai Das residence where Balai is the reader of Jibankrishna's (Diamond) Bengali book 'Dharma-O-Anubhuti' (Religion and Realization).

He narrated his own experience thus:

I took initiation from a preceptor (Guru) in Vaishab Cult. But I never got peace in me.

After attending the reading center for a few days I had an experience. I was going by bus from Sealdah Station to Babughat. Within the bus, I fell into a trance and saw the sky of dark color. Then gradually that dark color was transformed into silver color and from that silver color bright rays were coming out. From those rays, a bright light came to me. I noticed that the light was coming out from Sri Ramkrishna and Balai. Far away was seen the bright sun and within the sun was seen a man with a bare upper body and wearing a dhoti. He had short hair cutting. Then he said, 'You have gone to so many places. Have you got the truth? Come, let me show you God.' Suddenly I saw that a bulky, black-complexioned man with two horns on his head and holding a spear in his hand came out of my body, and instantly that person in the sun beheaded him. Thereafter I saw endless water within my naval region. The moonbeam fell on it and the water taking the silver color was glittering. The next time it was seen that a bee with a humming sound was continuously moving from the naval region to the mid-eyebrows and vice-versa. At this moment the bus conductor called me and I woke up from my trance. I saw that the bus became empty as all the passengers got down. I was merged with a perpetual joy. Later on when Balai showed me the photo of Jibankrishna I recognized that I saw him in my dream.

[The seer saw Jibankrishna in the sun which is mentioned in Upanishads written thousands of years ago. The black-complexioned man was Demon or animal passion, who was destroyed by Brahma or the Supreme Being and then he showed God to the seer.]

Jugal Chadra Ghorui of Paikpara, Kolkata is a regular listener in the Tala Park reading the center where Balai Das reads regularly Diamond's Bengali book 'Dharma-O-Anubhuti' (Religion and Realization). Within a few days, he saw Diamond in dreams, which he narrated thus:

One day in the month of November 2007 I saw in a dream a bright blue sky and in it the sun was illuminating bright rays. Inside the sun Jibankrishna was seated in a posture as seen in the photograph. My body became light and like a bird, I was flying in the sky. Suddenly from my mid-eye-brow, a very minute bright red ball came out and merged with Jibankrishna sitting in the sun. My dream went off.

[The dream indicates thus: Diamond in the sun proved Upanishads to be true. They also described the man in the sun as 'Brahma' or Supreme Being. Then it showed that the soul of the seer is the soul of Diamond and such is the case of every human being. This is also mentioned in Upanishads where they have mentioned that the soul of the attainer of Godhood becomes the soul of mankind which is 'one'.]

Snehamaya Ganguly of Sriniketan, Birbhum district of West Bengal State, India narrates his dream thus: Far away from me I saw the sun rising and the form of Jibankrishna inside it was visible. Holding a baby on my lap, I was calling everybody very loudly, and running towards him I put down the baby from my lap. Then the form of Jibankrishna in the sun vanished. In front of me, I saw a wall and a dried flower garland floating in the air came to me and automatically encircled my neck. When I woke up I saw that I was reciting the name 'Jibankrishna'.]

Mrs. Minati Das, a 60 years old listener of Barisha Reading Centre, Kolkata has narrated her dream thus :

On March 4, 1999, I saw that I was standing in front of a house and the waves of the sea were striking the house. It was then becoming dawn. I looked at the sky to see the rising sun. Suddenly I saw that the morning sun was rising and Jibankrishna was seated within the sun. I kept on looking at him and then my dream was off.

[The person in the sun is mentioned in Isa Upanishad as Parama Brahma or the Supreme Self.]

Jibankishna In The Sun As An Unknown Person

Ms. Pratima Halder from Barisha Reading Centre, Kolkata has narrated a dream thus :

In the year 1999, I saw the sun just like a huge plate. Inside that, a burning earthen lamp was set. The flame was high rising and inside the flame, the face of Jibankrishna was seen.

During these dreams, I had neither known him nor seen his photo. After seeing his photo I recognized it.

PART 3 THE IMMORTALITY OF JIBANKRISHNA OR DIAMOND

The man who does not desire – He who is without desire, who is freed from desire, whose desire is satisfied, whose desire is the Soul – his breaths do not depart. Being very Brahma, he goes to Brahma.

On this point there is a verse:

"When are liberated all the desires
That lodge in one's heart,

"That God, the All-worker, the Great Soul,
Ever seated in the heart of creatures,
Is framed by the heart, by the thought, by the mind –
They who know That becomes immortal". [4.17]

Svetasvatara Upanishad

CHAPTER 1 THE IMMORTALITY OF HUMAN BEING

In the month of February 11, 1959, Jibankrishna discussed with the listeners present in his room about the immortality of human beings as such:

"Sri Aravinda while describing a quatrain of Rig Veda has used the term 'Immortality' thus: "To discover and realize immortal life in a body subject to death and constant mutation. To realize this, four states take place: (1) God; (2) Light; (3) Freedom; (4) Immortality.

Now see, these were the versions of the Vedic Rishis (Sages) long, long time ago. But has he become immortal who has translated it?

See, I have not read it before, but a long time ago I told you that I shall live forever with this physical body. What is the proof that the Soul or Atma is immortal? Unless there is the existence of the physical body, who will prove that Atma is immortal? This physical body is another form of Atma. When one lives forever with his physical body, the immortality of Atma will be proved, otherwise, 'Atma is immortal' is merely a hypothesis.

But one thing I have understood is that as in a human brain there is the existence of the cells of joy and sorrow, light and darkness, in the same manner, there is the existence of death and immortality. As the same cell functions for sorrow and joy, light and darkness, in the same fashion the same cell functions for death and immortality. See for example, when a man gets enjoyment, does he feel sorrow at the same time? No. So long human beings have been worshiping death. They have forgotten immortality. The prayers of the Vedic sages, 'Take me from death to immortality' remain academic. But now this is not merely a prayer. This has manifested in reality though in individualism. Where is the proof? If I become immortal, otherwise this is merely a hypothesis.

But keep in mind that a human brain possesses the cell of both immortality and death and if it functions spontaneously it will be proved, otherwise not."

Brihad Aranyaka Upanishad has described as such:

This mankind is honey for all things, and all things are honey for this mankind. This shining, immortal Person who is in this mankind, and, with reference to oneself, this shining, immortal Person who exists as a human being – he is just this Soul, this Immortal, this Brahma, this All. (2.5.13)

THE IMMORTALITY OF JIBANKRISHNA

November 16 – 23, 1958.

Jibankrishna discussed one day:

I am saying that I shall live forever. Vedas have mentioned – Free of sorrow, death, and disease. And this 'forever' means unless the whole human race sees my form. Why I am saying so? Death is the prejudice of every human being and it is destined. But now I have become free of it. The meaning of birth and death run simultaneously. But I am not accepting it. I live forever with this form, otherwise, before death, I shall say that all these are nothing but hoaxes. You may charge me then, what are all these? I will say then, 'Yes, this is one, so you see my form.'

Now you are the authorities of all these, and it is true. You bless me so that this becomes universal. I want to get the whole human race within me.

People may call me insane. But actually, I am in a cool brain. I am explaining this matter with logic, and this is mentioned in 'Kaibalya' and 'Bibhutipad' (written thousands of years ago).

We cannot still conceive the final conclusion of this phenomenon, though, there must be an effect of it, and in the future, we can see it. When there is work there must be the ultimate effect.

"Here a gentleman named Moni came and said that he saw me with shaved head twenty-five years back sitting at Chetlahat (a marketplace at Kolkata). At first, he could not recognize, but when I shaved my head one day, he said, 'I have seen you with such shaved head sitting at Chetlahat. 'Chetlahat means the place of universal consciousness. It indicated that I would be in existence in this form as the consciousness of every human being forever and this is the explanation of my immortality".

[Katha Upanishad has mentioned:

Brahma in Form is Higher Than Formless Brahma

"Higher than the un-manifest, however, is the Person (Purusha),
All-pervading and without any mark whatever,
Knowing which, a man is liberated,
And goes to immortality". [6.8]

The Passage of The Soul From The Body to Eternity Leads to Immortality

"There are a hundred and one channels of the heart,
One of these passes up to the crown of the head.
Going up by it, one goes to immortality.
The others are for departing in various directions". (6.16)]

CHAPTER 2 SEEING JIBANKRISHNA IN HIS PHYSICAL BODY AFTER HIS DEATH

[Jibankishna is still seen in dreams and physical body even after his demise in 1967 AD among innumerable people not only in India but in many parts of the world being God-the-Preceptor of the seers, guiding and teaching them the mystery of yoga within a human body and thus they get the supreme knowledge to become one with the humanity]

Nagendra Basu Roy from Baguiati Reading Center, Kolkata has narrated how he saw Jibankrishna in his Physical body.

I was suddenly attacked by a serious illness. The doctor advised for surgery. Thereafter, I was admitted to Hospital. My operation would start at 2-00 A.M. My lower body was made paralyzed by injection. I could see the operation through T. V. and all the time I was reciting the name of Jibankrishna. The operation was successfully done. After 2-3 days the nurse was feeding me lunch. At this moment I saw that wearing dhoti and punjabi a gentleman was standing behind the curtain, on his head, there was a white cap like a Muslim. After some time it flashed in my mind, oh! He was Jibankrishna! Then and there he disappeared. I realized that he appeared in the physical body

[Thus even after 43 years of his death, Jibankrishna appears in the physical body on many occasions proving the immortality of his form which was also mentioned in Upanishads written thousands of years ago.]

Mrs. Savitri Paswan from Beleghata Reading Centre has narrated a dream.

One day in the year 2004 my mind was in a great depression sitting in a place I was weeping. Suddenly in my open eyes, I saw that on the throne of Lord Shiva's idol Jibankrishna jumped and sat on the throne. From his naval region light was emerging filling the whole room. So long I was weeping in reality, but after seeing him in reality my mind was full of divine joy.

[The seer actually saw it in her half-conscious state. It also indicates that Jibankrishna is himself Lord Shiva who is the insignia of 'oneness'].

Ms. Sohini Sen from Barisha Reading Center, Kolkata has narrated her vision in reality as such:

It was the month of March 2006. One day I had a conflict in my family. Then at 11-45 AM I started reading the Electricity chapter of physics. Suddenly I saw that the form of Jibankrishna in meditation posture was floating over the book. It was very colorful. After floating over the book the form flew to the sky and then disappeared. The same scene was repeated 4-5 times. I saw it in reality.

Gautam Goswami from Charupalli (Bolpur, Birbhum district, West Bengal, India) has narrated his experiences. In the year 1991, I was going to see my clock to know the time. I was holding a hurricane. I saw in my open eyes a man inside the clock. He resembled Jibankrishna. I was scared and came back. When next time I again went there I could see nothing.
[The seer saw Jibankrishna as 'Time' because the clock is the symbol of time. Time is merged in Atma or Soul. Jibankrishna's form is Atma.]

Ms. Mousumi Dhar from Abinashpur, Birbhum has narrated how she saw Jibankrishna in the physical body in reality. Her narration is as such:
On July 24, 1998, I was returning from Seuri to Abinashpur by sitting on a motorcycle on the backside of my husband who was driving. It was raining very heavily and he could not see the surroundings well. Once the bike jumped falling into the hole. I was raised higher up on the bike. I was fearing that now I would fall on the ground and my waist

would be broken. But strangely I saw that Jibankrishna made me sit on the bike by holding my waist. I was not harmed or injured. The next time I had confusion about whether I saw it properly. Was it not my hallucination? Probably Jibankrishna within me understood my confusion. But again strangely the same incident happened. The bike jumped due to falling into a hole and I was raised up high, and then Jibankrishna made me sit on the bike.
This time my disbelief was removed. Thinking about the grace of Jibankrishna I returned home crying throughout my journey.

Ms. Pranati Gayen has narrated a vision in reality. On January 8, 2001, at noon I was planning to conduct my own dance program on the stage. Suddenly a vision appeared in front of me. I saw that on the hanging corridor of a two-storied house Jibankrishna was standing with a mild smile. In the background, there was a blue curtain with ornamental work and from there a bright illumination was coming out. After a few seconds, the vision disappeared.
[God-the-Preceptor thus shows his grace on the seer.]

Ashis Karmakar from Gargaria, Bolpur has narrated his vision in reality thus:

In the month of February 2003 one day I was listening to the reading of Jibankrishna's Bengali book "Dharma-O-Anubhuti" (Religion and Realization in English).

At the end of the reading, everybody touched the book on the head and Rudra babu kept the book on a drum. My notice fell on the outline of Jibankrishna printed on the book. I saw that the outline became alive in the form of Jibankrishna. I noticed that the two front teeth were slightly bigger and the eyes were large. The bright light was coming out from him. But strangely I never saw his photo. For a long time, I kept on looking at him with great charm. Then the vision was off.

[The effect of listening to the reading fell upon the seer and he got the grace of Jibankrishna.]

Biswanath Chatterjee from Charupalli (Birbhum district of West Bengal state, India) has narrated his experience of how he saw Jibankrishna in the physical body.

It was the year. For a few days I was hearing about Jibankrishna I attended the reading center of Sridhar Ghosh's residence for listening to the reading of Jibankrishna's Bengali book 'Dharma –O- Anubhuti'

(Religion and Realization in English version). I enjoyed reading this book and at the same time, I was surprised to hear that he is seen in dreams, trances, etc.

In the meanwhile one day, I had a strange experience in the reading center. Snehamay was reading and all of us were listening. At that moment I saw in my open eyes that Jibankrishna with a bare upper body and wearing dhoti was sitting beside Snehamay. I was once looking at him and again listening to the reading. It continued a number of times and then he disappeared.

Ms. Baishakhi Mondal is a 13 years old girl and studies in class seven. She attends the reading at Bolpur Reading Centre. She narrated her experiences thus:

In the year 1990, one night I saw in my dream that Jibankrishna transformed me into a decade leaf of a tree and flying in space. I began to round the earth with great joy. Then my dream was off.

Baishakhi also narrated her strange experiences in reality and dream as such:

In the year 1991, for a few days, I was experiencing some strange matters in broad daylight. Some of our friends were seeing Jibankrishna in the physical body. Sometimes he was emerging from bamboo leaves, sometimes from flowering plants, and sometimes from flowers. One night I dreamed that Jibankrishna emerged from an iron rod. He said, 'I exist with everybody and so it happens like this.' I said, 'Iron rod is an inanimate object'. At that moment the iron rod spoke like a human being according to his instruction, and asked me, 'From where you are coming?' I answered, 'I have come from the same place from where you have come, that is from Jibankrishna'. Then and their iron rod was transformed into Jibankrishna's photo.

2002 A.D.

Kaushik Ghosh, 14 years old and a student of class nine narrated his experience of how he saw Jibankrishna in a waking state as such:

One day I was returning home alone after attending the Reading Centre at Charupalli, Bolpur. The lane was dark in the night. I was scared and remembered the name 'Jibankrishna'. Then I saw that Jibankrishna wearing a white dhoti and with a bare body was coming behind me. So without any fear, I went home. Entering into the home I thought to see Jibankrishna again and so I looked at him, but could not see him after coming out of the home. Next

moment I ran towards the Reading Centre at Biplab's house and narrated my vision to all the listeners.
[Jibankrishna protects thus all the devotees.]

Ms. Bisakha Chatterjee from Charupalli Reading Centre of Jambuni, Bolpur, narrated her experience in waking state how she got the grace of Jibankrishna:
One night (23.9.2001) before my gall-bladder operation I saw in a dream that I was lying on the lap of Jibankrishna for the whole night. I had no fear.
The next day during operation my sense came back and saw that young Jibankrishna was doing my operation. The doctors were discussing among themselves saying, 'Can the operation be done with such Ultra-Sonography? The case is very complicated.' Suddenly I said, 'Do not worry. I have my God with me. Complete the operation without any tension'. They exclaimed 'Oh, the patient got back sense! Be silent, do not talk'. They started again and the operation was completed easily.
When I think about the grace of Jibankrishna, I cannot fathom it.

Sukumar Moitra goes to the residence (Santragachi, Howrah) of Deb Kumar Choudhury companion of Jibankrishna to listen to his reading of JIbankrishna's Bengali book 'Dharma-O-Anubhuti' (English version 'Religion and Realization).

He narrated his experience of how he saw Jibankrishna in the physical body and in a dream.

On January 30, 1995, I was walking on the road for going to my office. Suddenly I saw a rickshaw coming behind me. As soon as it came near me, it stopped. Turing my face behind I saw that Jibankrishna was seated on the Rickshaw. He had a fair complexion, a very strongly built body.

The rickshaw driver got down from the rickshaw, but it moved automatically to a certain distance. While moving, the nuts of the rear tire scratched my leg and tore a portion of my cloth. I became agitated and wanted to scold the rickshaw driver. But all of a sudden all my agitation was removed by some unknown cause. So I told the driver, 'What has happened is predestined. What will you do? Don't mind. Go! But my cloth is torn. I have only two clothes. How shall I manage'? I noticed that Jibankrishna was seated on the rickshaw silently.

While I approached a certain distance, I realized that all these incidents happened in my half-conscious state, nothing happened in the physical eye.

Reba Das

I Saw Unknown And unseen Jibankrishna in the Physical Body After His Death

Before I joined the Reading Center of Khardaha, 24-Parganas (N), West Bengal (India), I had so many strange experiences. Whenever I used to walk it seemed that somebody was walking with me at night. Even I used to feel his breathing, I could not see anybody, of course, I was never scared.

From my very childhood, I saw many divine dreams. Sometimes I told my mother about these dreams and she advised me saying, 'Tell the pond water or tell the trees', etc. Sometimes I used to see that I was reading religious books kept on the small table.

Once hearing my dreams one lady of Santinagar took me to a Reading Center where I met Mrs. Sova Pal as a reader. On that very day during the recitation of hymns, I saw in trance Sri Ramkrishna wearing a black coat and trousers. He was standing touching my body. During this time I became half-conscious and one of the listeners was massaging my chest. After a while, I got back my full sense. Henceforth I started going to the Reading Center. I used to hear many dreams of all the listeners and everybody used to narrate how they say Jibankrishna in dreams. But I had this question always, who is this Jibankrishna. I have heard the names of Sri Ramkrishna, mother Sarada and Swami Vivekananda, but I never agreed about the Godhood of Jibankrishna.

Once one listener sister Anjali and I had gone to a market and saw an old gentleman standing very near to me watching the market area. For a few seconds I looked at him twice but for the third time, I could not see him.

Thereafter due to some unavoidable circumstances some of us e.g., Anjali, Purnima, Sankari, Rinku, Chandana, and Kalpana were detached from the Reading Centre and then came in touch with Mrs. Biva Das, a reader of Baguiati Reading Center, Kolkata.

Once I went to Betaitala, Howrah (where Jibankrishna used to like for about a year in his last days) and gradually got in touch with Basudeb Pal, Samir Banerjee, Nirmal Mondal, Asim Biswas, Dhiren Mondal, Arun Ghosh, etc. who were the companions of Jibankrishna and I got a divine peace in my life.

The most amazing incident happened in my life when on August 15, 2011, at Nirmal Mondal's residence in a gathering one young boy came and narrated a strange experience. When he was drinking water before taking a cup of tea, an aged gentleman wearing a dhoti up to his knee with a towel on his shoulder and bare upper body was telling him, 'oh, you know that before taking tea drinking water is necessary'! The boy said, 'will you take tea'? He said, 'will you? Yes, I will take.' So the boy gave him a cup of tea and offered a biscuit. But the gentleman denied and then asked, 'where are you going?' The boy said, ' I am going to uncle Nirmal's residence'. He said, 'yes, you go, you will get enjoyment there'.

When the boy gave the money to the shopkeeper and turned his head, he could not find any trace of the gentleman.

Brother Samir was reading the Gospel of Sri Ramkrishna. He asked the boy, 'From where that gentleman had come?' Everybody kept silent in the room. Instantly an utterance came out from my mouth, 'He came out of his body and again entered into his body.' Then and there it flashed in my mind that the same case happened in my life in the market. That old man came out from my body and again entered into my body!.

It was strange that from that day my philosophy of life completely changed having numerous realizations.

After a few days when I went to brother Sridhar's residence at Bolpur and saw a photo of Jibankrishna, I was overwhelmed with surprise that I saw him in the market quite a few months ago.

I had a similar experience once when I was going to my father's house at Jirat near Kolkata. I was standing at the railway station and was thinking if I miss the Katwa local, I would be in great trouble. Suddenly, I saw that a gentleman was seated beside me. He asked me, 'Mother, where you will go'? I said, 'Jirat'. He said, 'I shall go to Guptipara to avail a train for Salar.

Just at the moment, Barrackplore Local train entered into the platform and I got up on the train. After reaching Barrackpore station I got down on the platform where Salar local was supposed to come. There I saw that the same gentleman was seated on a bench. He told me to sit beside him, but I did not sit. Then he said, 'within two seconds the train will come.' And actually, within two seconds the train came. When I turned I did not see that man.

However, after reaching my destined place I finished my work and returned home. At that moment I realized that the gentleman was Jibankrishna.

After this incident, I engaged myself only in Jibankrishna's affairs and nothing else.

Deblina Kundu resides at Howrah Town near Kolkata. Her maternal grandfather Basudeb Roy was a regular companion of Diamond from a young age. Deblina heard many times about Diamond from Basudeb though she never saw Diamond physically. As Basudeb was her grandpa, she used to consider Diamond as her grandpa. Deblina had some ideas about Diamond's figure as his photograph was kept hanging against the wall.

Deblina narrated two very interesting incidents that happened in her life at an early age which she never forgot. The first incident happened about 18 years ago when her age was about 2-2.5years old in the year 1985-86. One day she was lying on her grandpa's cot. After a while, she decided to get down but couldn't due to her height. Suddenly Diamond, coming out of the photo held her and put her on the floor. Later, seeing Deblina moving on the floor everybody was surprised and asked, 'How did you get down from such a high cot?' she said, ' Why? That grandpa came out of the photo and put me down on the floor.'

The second incident happened when she was 4years old. She was then a student of St Thomas school at Howrah in the nursery section.

One day, the teacher did not come to the class at the scheduled time. As a monitor, she became in charge of the class, but could not control anybody. So all became out of control and made a great noise within the class. Nobody was listening to her. Suddenly Deblina saw that on the teacher's platform goddess Kali, Sri Ramkrishna and (as she mentioned) grandpa of the photo(Diamond) appeared and scolded the students so loudly that everybody kept silent at once. Within a moment they disappeared. After coming back home she narrated this incident to her mother who after long years told me for my magazine. Deblina never forgets that scene.]

CHAPTER 3 IMMORTALITY OF JIBANKRISHNA – HIS APPEARANCE IN DREAMS AFTER DEATH AS AN UNKNOWN MAN

I saw Jibankrishna) in dreams through Reading Center before seeing his photo

Satyavati Debi

I started attending the reading center at Santragachi, Howrah (West Bengal State, India) where Jibankrishna's

Bengali book ‘Dharma-O-Anubhuti’ used to be read regularly. For a few months, I could not attend. Then one night I saw a dream: My third son-in-law Sachin has come to our house from Allahabad. I was then in the kitchen. My grandson came and told me, ‘Grandma, uncle has come.’ I hurriedly came out of the kitchen and saw one gentleman sitting on the cot was talking to Sachin. I asked Sachin, ‘Who is he? I don’t recognize him.’ Sachin said, ‘My maternal uncle.’ I saw that he had a bare upper body. Then I said, ‘Let me make a cup of tea.’ Sachin said, ‘He never eats from others.’ My dream was off.

Later on, one day going to the reading center I saw Jibankrishna’s photo and recognized him to be the same person I saw in my dream.

[Sri Ramkrishna used to say that maternal uncle is God and He is for all. Here the seer had a vision of God and at the same time gets Jibankrishna as her God-the-Preceptor.]

I saw Jibankrishna in a dream before seeing his photo

Mrs. Chapala Pal

I am a regular listener of Santragachi (Howrah, West Bengal, India) reading center where Jibankrishna’s Bengali book 'Dharma-O-Anubhuti' (Religion and Realization in the English version) is read regularly. After a few days, I saw in my dream that one gentleman was seated with closed eyes. He had a bare upper body, a fair complexion with a short hairstyle. He was also very robust. My daughter, granddaughter and I was offering flowers to him. My dream was off.

Later on, going to the reading center I saw Jibankrishna's photo and saw that he was the same man whom we offered flowers in my dream. I am an old woman of 72 years old and strangely I got the blessings of God by his grace.

I saw this dream sometime in the month of March
1971.

How Jibankrishna was introduced through dream

Pramilabala Dasi

It was about the year 1967. I used to go to a Reading Center of Sitalatala, Howrah (West Bengal, India). But could not understand anything and thought what were they discussing! Then this Center was closed and a new Center was opened at the residence of Krishna Samanta at Shibpur, Howrah. I started attending that Center, though I knew nothing about Jibankrishna.

In my first dream (July – Aug 1967) I saw that brother Krishnadhan showing a gentleman was telling me, 'This is Jibankrishna'. And my dream was off.

After a few days, I again saw in my dream that Sri Ramkrishna and Jibankrishna were lying side by side. Then my dream was off.

[By the grace of Jibankrishna the seer saw him in a dream before seeing him in reality. In the second dream it was shown to the seer that both Sri Ramkrishna and Jibankrishna are identical.]

I saw Jibankrishna in dreams before seeing his photo

Vidyut Kumar Das

Sometime in 1978 A.D, I saw a dream. I had gone to see a movie with someone. As it was about to start late, I roamed here and there. On the road, I purchased a sweet and ate. Seeing a religious preceptor of one of my friends I was going to bow down to him, but just at that moment somebody held me with his left arm and made me sit on his left side. My dream went off.

Later on, when I saw a photo of Jibankrishna in the Reading Center, I recognized that I saw him in my dream.

[Here the seer got Jibankrishna as his God-the-Preceptor.]

I saw Jibankrishna's house in dreams before seeing it in reality

Raghunath Prasad settled in Bengal from U. P. (India) a long time back. He used to attend the Reading Center at Salikha, Howrah to listen to the reading of Diamond's Bengali book 'Dharma-O-Anubhuti' (English version is Religion and Realization).

After attending the Reading Center for a few days he had two dreams which are as such :

Sitting on the portico of a house Jibankrishna was rubbing mustard oil on his body. When I went to him he gave me some 'muri' (rice roasted in hot sand). But as I denied he told me in the Hindi language to eat it. So after eating I went with him to take bath. As he was taking a bath lifting water from the well. Then my dream went off.

Later on when I went to his residence at Betaitala, Howrah I became surprised to see his house. The same house I saw in my dream.

I saw Jibankrishna in a dream without seeing his photo

Mrs. Madhuri Devi

It was sometime in the year 1979. One day I went to Belur Math (Howrah district, West Bengal, India) and after listening to the hymns (devotional song in Sanskrit) in the evening I came out and suddenly felt a trance like sensation. It seemed to me as if I was alone there, no trace of any human being. Then I saw Sri Ramkrishna standing there with the book 'The Gospel of Sri Ramkrishna in his hand. He was asking me, well, you worship so many deities, but adjacent to your house, there is a Reading Center and you don't go there'! Suddenly I got back my sense and saw the crowd around me.

Even after this realization, I could not go to the Reading Center.

Then it happened one day that I went to listen to the devotional songs at a Doctor's house near our residence on one Sunday as usual. There I listened to the reading of Jibankrishna's) Bengali book 'Dharma-O-Anubhuti' (Religion and Realization in the English version) and the Gospel of Sri Ramkrishna' and became impressed by the reading of Radharaman Chatterjee.

Being introduced to him I came to know that he used to read every Friday evening at the residence of Krishna Mohan Banerjee just beside our residence. Hence forth I started going there every Friday.

Then one day I saw in my dream a gentleman sitting beside my bed, though there was no conversation. His body color was reddish. Then my dream was off.

The next time I went to the Reading Center, I saw the photo of Jibankrishna and recognized that I saw him in my dream.

I saw Jibankrishna in a dream without seeing his photo

Mrs. Bijalibala Bhattacharjee of Ketugram, Katoa (Burdwan District, West Bengal, India) has narrated her experiences after attending a Reading Center where Diamond's (Jibankrishna) Bengali book 'Dharma-O-Anubhuti' (Religion and Realization in the English version) is read on regular basis.

February 20, 1972.

About a year ago, Sushanta Banerjee started reading Jibankrishna's book at the residence of Tarakbrahma Chatterjee. Listening to the reading on the very first day I saw a dream :

With a bare upper body and wearing a dhoti, an aged man came to me. He had a black and white beard and eyebrows with short hair cut. He was also holding a stick in his hand and told me, 'I am going to have a tour round the world. Mother, give me a glass of water.' It was then noon time and I was cooking. I took a glass of water and searched for some sweets. I was thinking how could I give him only water! But he said, 'See, you may have sugar cake inside the cupboard.' I noticed a huge cupboard of sugar cake inside the room. I broke them into pieces and after mixing them with water gave him in a glass. After drinking he became satisfied and told me, 'You have given me great peace. You also drink this.' Then he uttered 'Om Peace! Om Peace! Om Tatsat!' Patting on my head he blessed me and my dream was off.

When next day I told Sushanta about this dream he said that had seen Jibankrishna who blessed me in a dream and gave me peace. And it is a fact that Jibankrishna is giving me peace through dreams in various ways. After a few days when Sushanta showed me the photo of Jibankrishna, I recognized him to see the same man in the dream.

I saw Jibankrishna in a dream without knowing or seeing him before

Nakuleswar Bhattacharjee

On one Saturday of September, 1967, I saw in a dream that a gentleman had come to the corridor of our house and was looking t me. It was then 11-00 P.M. The gentleman was tall, stout figure with a vanish sandal on feet and wearing a black stripped dhoti and Punjabi on the upper body. He was covered with a Kashmiri Sal (winter garment). Seeing him I tried to shout 'who are you', but at that time I became half-paralyzed and my voice was almost choked. Having no answer from him I thought him to be a robber and again tried to answer. Then I saw that his dresses started to be transformed into height gradually and ultimately he was transformed into a great light and disappeared. My dream was off. Thereafter, at the beginning of 1970, I was introduced to a gentleman named Smarajit Mondal. He gave me a magazine 'Manikya'. I saw in that magazine that innumerable people used to see a man named Jiban Krishna in dreams etc. I told Mr. Mondal about my dream and he showed me a photograph. As soon as I saw it I recognized him as the same person I saw in my dream. He was Jiban Krishna himself.

I saw Jibankrishna in a dream as an unknown man

Sanjay Kumar Sen

It was a Monday on July 20, 1970. On that day I brought from one of my uncles Dhirendra Nath Roy a Bengali book 'Dharma-o-Anubhuti' (Religion and Realization) written by

Diamond picked up in the street. Previously I read a Bengali magazine 'Manikya' from him and after seeing the advertisement of the book 'Dharma-o-Anubhuti' out of curiosity, I brought this book.

I had a regular practice of reading books before sleeping at night. Last night I read a part of the Bible. Tonight I started reading this new book. After reading for a while I slept and had a strange dream. I had gone to a house with two rooms. I saw that in one of the rooms my uncle was cooking vegetables. I asked him, 'Oh, you are cooking yourself! He said, 'I cook myself and eat vegetarian food'.

There was another room beside that room and in between, there was a swing door. As soon as I went to that room, my uncle told me not to enter there. But in the meantime, pushing that door I stood in front of that room. Looking inside, I was puzzled and my whole body shivered. The door was dark and a hazy form of a human being was seated inside the room with light illuminating all rounds. Here my dream was off. I couldn't find any explanation for my dream even by reading this book. I got great joy after reading but didn't get any clue about my dream. Then one day I went to my uncle and narrated my dream. It was a strange thing that for a few days he was having vegetarian food which I didn't know. He explained my dream and said that I saw him in the dream by his grace.

[The form within the dream was the same as on the cover of the book 'Dharma-o-Anubhuti.]

I saw Jibankrishna in a dream without knowing or seeing him in the photo before

Arun Kumar Basu

For a few days, I read the Bengali magazine 'Manikya' and saw a dream.

The dream was thus: I was standing on the roof of another house and saw below many small houses. Suddenly, I shouted 'Thief! Thief! Hearing my shout many people came out and three of them stood below. One of them got up the roof. There was a tunnel beside my house and through this tunnel, a man jumped on the ground. I had a long stick which I threw against him but did not touch him. The man looked at me. I saw him as a tall, strongly built man with a shaved head. I saw so many people but never saw such a man. I feared breaking my own legs on jumping. So I wanted to get down through the back side and here my dream was off.

Later on when I saw a photograph from Sarojit Mondal (A regular companion of Jibankrishna) I was confirmed that by hi grace Jiban Krishna appeared in my dream. But I was so astonished when I through that I had done nothing, yet why I got his grace and saw him!

Seeing young Jibankrishna in a dream as an unknown man

Ms. Sarama Mondal of Sankteria, Burdwan (Wet Bengal, India) has narrated how she saw young aged Jiban Krishna in a dream without seeing his photo before. Her narration is such :

On May 21, 2009, I saw in my dream that I was taking boiled rice in my lunch. At this moment a young boy of about 19 years old wearing dhoti and bare upper body came and asked, 'Let us go, to the Reading Centre'. I said, 'Let me finish my supper'. At that moment uncle Snehamay (Reader of the Reading Centre) came and told him, 'you go and I am taking her to the center.' The boy was happy and went away. When I woke up I realized that he was Jibankrishna of his young age as seen in the photograph.

Seeing Jibankrishna in a dream as an unknown man

Mrs. Ranu Bose from Dhakuria Reading Centre, Kolkata has narrated how she saw Jiban Krisna or Diamond in a dream without seeing his photo before. Her narration is such :

One day somebody asked me how could I know about Jibankrishna. I said, 'see, when I became widow, my mind was very much disturbed. I was going to the office, during my regular job, yet my mind was suppressed and disturbed. During that time one lady named Niva used to work at our office. One day she gave me a Bengali magazine 'Manikya' and said, 'Read this book, I think you may get peace'. So after coming back home after my work I started reading the magazine.

on that very night, I saw a dream. I saw that a gentleman of very strong and stout health, wearing dhoti and Punjabi was standing at the door resting his two hands on the door. But he was silent. I was feeling a divine joy after seeing that gentleman. Then my dream was off. The next day when I went to the office and narrated the dream to Niva, she said, 'You have seen Jibankrishna'. Later on, I identified Jibankrishna with his photograph. Thereafter I saw Jibankrishna in dreams many times. Still, whenever I remember the first dream I feel great divine joy.

Arindam Mukherjee of Dhakuria Reading Center, Kolkata narrated a strange dream.

On January 1, 2009, in the evening dream, I saw that a middle-aged gentleman was seated in the posture of meditation. He was strong and stout, having short hair on his head, fair-complexioned childish looking. A bright light was emerging from his body. I couldn't recognize him. My dream was then off.

Later on, when I narrated the dream to Ms. Dipali, she showed me a photograph of Jiban Krishna (Diamond), and I recognized him to be the same man seen in my dream. Thus I got Jiban Krishna as my god-the-Preceptor

Sailendra Mohan Saha of Sodepur, 24-Parganas (N), (West Bengal, India) has narrated how he saw Jibankrishna in a dream without seeing his photo before. He narrated thus:

On May 31, 2011, I saw in my dream that I was returning from a fair with all my family members. The road was all along a river side with a steep slope. Out of curiosity seeing others I also got down the slope and touched the river water. But suddenly I could not see anybody there. I was thinking about how to get up and began to cry shedding tears. I was praying to god, 'Oh Lord, how can I get up on the bank. Have I to give up my life here'? All of a sudden I saw a man wearing dhoti up to his knee, head wrapped with tape and holding a lantern and a long stick saying to me, Here is the way, come up'. He showed me the way with a lantern. I saw the earthen steps going up from the river. I made a sigh of relief. But couldn't see him anymore. The dream was off.

Later on, seeing Jibankrishna's photo I realized that the man in my dream was Jibankrishna himself.

How Jibankrishna's introduction was obtained in the second dream

Mr. Sudeshna Sarkar from Sakherbazar, Kolkata has narrated how she got Jiban Krishna's introduction in the succeeding dream.

One night in the month of May 2009, my old friends and I were sitting on the front portico of uncle Ramen's residence. I saw a man coming from a distant place towards us. He wore a white dhoti and Punjabi and his head was wrapped with a white handkerchief. Another friend of mine named Resmi was also coming towards us. When I went forward towards them the gentleman's hand touched my hand. With a smiling face, he looked at me and my body shivered. Then with a continuous look at me, he vanished gradually. My dream was off. I couldn't understand who the gentleman was.

The next day, in the noon time I saw another dream. This time I saw that I had gone to the residence of Moni Debnath. I asked him, 'Well, is he (whom I saw in my previous dream) God? Moni smiled and said, 'He is Jibankrishna'. The dream was off. [God gives his own introduction in such manner, sometimes through others, sometimes himself].

Seeing Jibankrishna in a dream as an unknown man and his own introduction

Mrs. Nanibala Das from Beleghata Reading Centre, Kolkata has narrated her dream thus:

I saw in my dream that three unknown persons entered into my room. I could not recognize any of them and looked at them with a great surprise. One of them told me, 'Hey, what are you looking? can't you recognize us'? Then showing one person he said, 'He is Ramkrishna', showing himself he said, 'I am Jibankrishna' and showing the third person he said, 'He is a devotee'. The dream was off.

[God-the-Preceptor thus introduces everything to the seer through the dreams.]

Seeing Jibankrishna in dreams without seeing his photo

Mrs. Smritikana Mukherjee is a listener of a Reading Centre and resides at Sonarpur, 24-Parganas (South), West Bengal, India. Here Jibankrishna's (Diamond) Bengali book 'Dharma-0-Anubhuti' (Religion and Realization in the English version) and the Gospel of Sri Ramkrishna are read regularly.

Smritikana has narrated her dream thus:

One day in the year 2004, I was lying on bed at my sister's residence in the night and dreamt that an old gentleman was seated near my head on the cot. It seemed that he was special and I began to feel great divine joy. Then my dream was off.

The next morning seeing a photo in my sister's house I asked, 'who is he? My sister said, 'He is Lord Jibankrishna'. I told her, 'This man appeared in my dream last night'.

[Like innumerable Ms. Smritikana is also a blessed one who got the grace of God and got Jibankrishna as her God-the-Preceptor.]

Seeing Jibankrishna in a dream as an unknown man and his own introduction

Mrs. Nanibala Das from Beleghata Reading Centre, Kolkata has narrated her dream thus:

I saw in my dream that three unknown persons entered into my room. I could not recognize any of them and looked at them with a great surprise. One of them told me, 'Hey, what are you looking? can't you recognize us'? Then showing one person he said, 'He is Ramkrishna', showing himself he said, 'I am Jibankrishna' and showing the third person he said, 'He is a devotee'. The dream was off.

[God-the-Preceptor thus introduces everything to the seer through the dreams.]

How Jibankrishna gave his own introduction through dreams

From Charabagan Reading Center (Howrah Town, West Bengal, India) Biswanath Ghosh narrated his strange experience in dreams.

On September 26, 1984, I saw in my dream that my wife, an aged widow, and I had gone to a house for listening to the reading of Diamond's (Jibankrishna) Bengali book

'Dharma-O-Anubhuti'. The reader was reading the Gospel of Sri Ramkrishna sitting on a cot facing the west side. The light was on. Inside the room, there was a wooden Almira and some old materials. The reader was a bit tall and healthy with a slight black complexion. After listening for a while we were about to come out. Then we saw that the reader started reading without uttering any sound, and we said, 'Let us go'. He answered, 'Yes, come again.' The dream was off.

This dream I narrated later on to some of the listeners. Hearing this Sailen De ad Mani Dey both asked, 'Did you guess that you had seen Jibankrishna'? I said, 'I can't say'.

Just the next day I again saw in my dream that same scene and somebody said, 'Oh! That was me'! It flashed in my mind, Oh! Then I saw Jibankrishna the previous day in my dream! Ten my dream was off.

[Thus Jibankrishna gave his own introduction in a dream.]

I saw Jibankrishna in a dream without seeing his photo

From Howrah Reading center Krishna Mohan Banerjee has narrated :

It happened in the year 1978. Once I intended very much to take initiation. But I couldn't decide from whom I should take it.

One day my wife told me, 'Why are you hankering after taking initiation? Pray to Sri Ramkrishna and recite his name.'

One day on my way to the office accidentally I met Radharam Chatterjee who was a reader of Jibankrishna's book at the residence of a gentleman. Within a few days, I went to his house and after listening to the reading of the Gospel of Sri Ramkrishna and about Jibankrishna I was highly satisfied. Then one day I took my wife there. Henceforth I started a Reading Center at my residence where every Friday reading of the Gospel of Sri Ramkrishna and Jibankrishna's Bengali book 'Dharma-O-Anubhuti' (Religion and Realization in the English version) has been continuing for the last three years. I have dreamed of both Jibankrishna and Sri Ramkrishna.

My dream:

I have not still seen the photo of Jibankrishna. One day I dreamed of a room that was very spacious with two doors. Entering through one door inside the room I saw a man sitting in front of the opposite wall and cutting fruit with a knife and a 7-8 years old girl was seated in front of him. Looking at the back of the gentleman I realized that he was very strongly built. Suddenly the girl ran inside and the gentleman followed her. The next moment returning inside the room he washed the knife in the basin and as soon as he turned, his white dhoti was about to be loosened from his waist. He held tightly the dhoti and said with a laugh, 'I have become old'! I said, 'No, No! Not at all, you are a heavy weight man so it is natural.' Then with a smiling look at me, he left the room. My dream was off.

When I told Radharaman about this dream, he said, 'you have seen Jibankrishna', and he showed me his photo. Then and there I recognized that I saw JIbankrishna in my dream.

How I heard Jibankrishna's voice a long time back without seeing or knowing him before

Bibhuti Santra attends regularly the Vijayananda Park, Reading Center and listens to the reading of Jibankrishna's (Diamond) Bengali book 'Dharma-O-Anubhuti' (Religion and Realization in the English version).

It was the incident on May 23, 2008. I went to a large gathering at the residence of Gopal Chandra Roy (a Companion of Jibankrishna), Betaitala, Howrah.

As usual, the books 'The Gospel of Sri Ramkrishna,' and 'Dharma-O-Anubhuti' were read continuously. The surrounding became very divine and peaceful. Everybody was listening with rapt attention. We couldn't hear any outside noise.

After a few hours it was interval, and then the C. D. on Jibankrishna's voice was played, though I could not guess before whose voice was going to be played.

But after a few minutes I was wondering, whose voice was this? About 25-26 years back I heard this same voice in my dream! During that time I had no idea who was Jibankrishna. But this voice came to me as an oracle in my worldly life. To-day I realized that the oracle came from Jibankrishna at that time.

Samaresh Chatterjee from Ilambazar, Birbhum (West Bengal, India) has narrated how he saw Jibankrishna or Diamond in dream without knowing or seeing him before. On May 23, 2011, I saw that by showing a photo in a room my wife was telling me, 'This is the picture of

Acharya Prafulla Chandra Roy'. But my son said, No, this is the photo of Jibankrishna. He is God. My dream was off. Next time when I went to Bolpur for attending the Reading Center, seeing a photo of Jibankrishna with beard I was overwhelmed with astonishment, oh, this photo I saw in my dream a few days ago! Yes, Acharya (Preceptor) is only God and none.

Ranita Maity is a 9 years old girl (In the year 2000) and is a listener at Barisha Reading Centre, Kolkata where the Bengali book of Jibankrishna 'Dharma-O-Anubhuti' (Religion and realization in English version) is read regularly. She has narrated how she saw Jibankrishna in a dream without seeing his photo before. Her dream as narrated by her is given.

On April 15, 2000, I was dreaming that Sri Ramkrishna was seated on a throne in my worship room. An old man was having a chit chat with him. He was unknown to me. In whichever direction I was looking I was noticing the portraits of Sri Ramkrishna. Then my dream was off.

Later on when I saw the photo of Jilbankrishna from Pabitra grandpa I recognized that the old man talking with Sri Ramkrishna in my dream was Jibnakrishna.

Jibankrishna in the sun as unknown person

Ms. Pratima Halder from Barisha Reading Center, Kolkata has narrated a dream thus :

In the year 1999 I saw the sun just like a huge plate. Inside that a burning earthen lamp was set. The flame was high rising and inside the flame the face of Jibankrishna was seen.

During these dreams I had neither known him nor seen his photo. After seeing his photo I recognized.

Ms. Sagarika Mukherjee from Barisha Reading Centre has narrated a dream where she saw Jibankrishna as unknown man. The narration is thus :

One day in the year 2004 saw in my dream that I was staying in a house with my husband and another fellow. At that moment a monk with red ochre dress was entering trough the main door. He had Gigantic figure, so tall to be touched with the door top. He entered into the room and with a great joy when I was going to bow down to him touching his feet, he said, 'Let it be, let it be.' I said, 'won't you take my pranam (bowing down)'? Hearing this he said, 'well, you do.' Then my dream was off.

Later on seeing a photo of Jibankrishna in my mother's (Mrs. Jyotsna Sarkar) room I realized that the monk in my dream was Jibankrishna.

[Monk – whose soul and body are separated. A real monk appears within the human beings and become their God-the-Preceptor.]

Ms. Ranjana Chakrabarty from Barisha Reading Center, Kolkata has narrated her dream as thus:

One day in the month of March, 2006, after going home I read Jibankrishna's Bengali book 'Dharma-O-Anubhuti' and then went to bed. Suddenly opening my eyes I saw that an aged gentleman of medium height was standing in front of me. He had short hair cutting but I could not remember who he was. Then I slept and dreamed that the same gentleman was telling me in smiling face, 'I am Jibankrishna. You have now achieved eight annas (50 percent of one rupee), later on it will be two rupees and then eight rupees. Then my dream was off. When I woke up, my whole body was full of Goosebumps with divine joy.

Jibakrishna in dream as an unknown man

Anandamayee Santra from a Reading Center of Howrah narrated how before seeing the photo of Jibankrishna she saw him in her dream. Her husband goes to listen to the reading of Diamond's Bengali book 'Dharma-O-Anubhuti' (Religion and Realization, English version).

On 21.03.2004 I saw in my dream in the night that I was walking on a road. I saw that beneath a big tree a fair complexioned strongly built person wearing a white cloth and bare upper body was having meditation. Seeing him my body shivered with joy. My head was down with great regard and I bowed to him. He opened his eyes and gave me some fruits. I saw that it was a papaya. My dream was off and I went on thinking who was that person? And why he gave me a papaya instead of so many fruits! I again slept and when I woke up in the morning, I narrated the dream to my husband. He showed me a photo and I was surprised that he was that person seen in my dream. Later on my husband told me that his name was Jibankrishna.

Jibankrishna in dream as an unknown man

Ms Malati Chakravarty has narrated her experience thus:

My mother-in-law is a regular listener at a Reading Center of Howrah Town where Diamond's Bengali book 'Dharma-O-Anubhuti' (Religion and Realization, English version) is read regularly. But without attending the reading she saw

Jibankrishna in her dream which she narrated thus. The construction of our new house was going on. A very strongly built gentleman wearing dhoti and Punjabi came and sat on a chair, and then took my son his lap. He began to give instructions about the construction. Then he told me to plant some coconut saplings. My dream was then off.

Waking up in the morning seeing Jibankrishna's photo I realized that I saw him in my dream. This was the first time he appeared in my dream.

Jibnkrishna in dream as an unknown man

From Phiringibagan Reading Center Bhairabi Dasi who resides at Katoa, Burdwan District of West Bengal, India,narrated her experiences as such:

I work as maid in different residences. Suddenly one night I saw in a dream that a middle aged, strong and stout gentleman wearing dhoti and Punjabi came to me with a married lady and told to work as a maid for Sadhan's residence.

Sadhan was known to me and later on I recognized Sadhan's mother Mrs. Bijalibala Dasi as the same lady seen in my dream, though I never saw her before.

However, I engaged myself as their maid and in due course of time I heard the amazing facts about the dreams of different people encircling Jibankrishna (Diamond) through reading his Bengali book Dharma-O-Anubhuti' (Religion and Realization in English version). One day I saw in my dream that a very healthy man with bare upper body, clean shaved face and head stood in my room and said, 'Don't be scared and worry. You will get wealth and you will have no lacking.' My dream went off.

Then one day I narrated my dreams to Sushanta Banerjee. He showed me a picture of Jibankrishna. I recognized him to be the same one seen in my previous dreams who gave me assurance of protection.

CPSIA information can be obtained
at www.ICGtesting.com
Printed in the USA
LVHW111039081122
732584LV00003BA/92

9 789356 754621